Cozy
Stash-Busting
KNITS

22 PATTERNS FOR HATS,
SCARVES, COWLS & MORE

Jen Lucas

Martingale®
Create with Confidence

Dedication

For my Tuesday-night knitting and crochet ladies. Thank you.

Cozy Stash-Busting Knits:
22 Patterns for Hats, Scarves, Cowls & More
© 2016 by Jen Lucas

Martingale®
19021 120th Ave. NE, Ste. 102
Bothell, WA 98011-9511 USA
ShopMartingale.com

Printed in China
21 20 19 18 17 16   8 7 6 5 4 3 2 1

Library of Congress Cataloging-in-Publication Data is available upon request.

ISBN: 978-1-60468-750-7

MISSION STATEMENT

We empower makers who use fabric and yarn to make life more enjoyable.

CREDITS

PUBLISHER AND CHIEF VISIONARY OFFICER
Jennifer Erbe Keltner

CONTENT DIRECTOR
Karen Costello Soltys

MANAGING EDITOR
Tina Cook

ACQUISITIONS EDITOR
Karen M. Burns

TECHNICAL EDITOR
Beth Bradley

COPY EDITOR
Marcy Heffernan

PRODUCTION MANAGER
Regina Girard

COVER AND INTERIOR DESIGNER
Adrienne Smitke

PHOTOGRAPHER
Brent Kane

ILLUSTRATOR
Linda Schmidt

Contents

Introduction

It's no secret that I have a thing for sock yarn—I've dedicated three books to it! I'm the self-proclaimed sock-yarn-shawl queen. But the reality is, I've been knitting with a whole lot of sock yarn. It's time for something new—and something bigger. Like many knitters, I love projects that are quick to knit. It's so satisfying to cast on for a new project and have a finished object a very short time later. I also love the idea of making larger projects, like shawls, in a thicker yarn. A big, thick, chunky shawl is the definition of cozy to me. Combining these elements seems right to me. A book full of stash-busting knits is the perfect break from all those sock-yarn shawls.

With a total of 22 patterns in this book, there's something for everybody. These accessory patterns range from shawls and scarves to mittens and headbands. The patterns are organized into three sections: DK-Weight Projects, Worsted- and Aran-Weight Projects, and Bulky and Super-Bulky Projects. Find something in the DK-weight section you want to make, but have a bulky yarn that you think will be perfect? No worries, as many of the patterns include "Make It Your Own!" tip boxes. These boxes contain tips and tricks on how to alter the pattern and, in some cases, information on yardage and stitch-count changes for a different weight of yarn. For even more information on this topic, see "Yarn Weight and Substitutions" on page 92.

I hope you enjoy diving into your stash and finding the perfect yarn for a quick and cozy knit!

~Jen

FLAVIA

Designed by author and knit by Melissa Rusk

This traditional top-down triangle shawl combines knit and purl stitches and simple shaping. The size of the shawl can easily be enlarged by adding extra repeats of the charts or by using a thicker yarn.

SKILL LEVEL: Intermediate

FINISHED MEASUREMENTS:
72" x 27"

MATERIALS

3 skeins of Breathless DK from Shalimar Yarns (75% superwash merino, 15% cashmere, 10% silk; 100 g; 270 yards) in color Damson ③

US size 6 (4.0 mm) circular needle, 32" cable or longer, or size required for gauge

2 stitch markers

Tapestry needle
Blocking supplies

GAUGE

16 sts and 24 rows = 4" in garter st

Gauge is not critical in this patt, but a different gauge will affect yardage and size of shawl.

PATTERN NOTES

Charts are on pages 10 and 11. If you prefer to follow written instructions for the charted material, see "Written Instructions for Charts" on page 8.

INSTRUCTIONS

Work garter-tab CO (page 90) as follows:

CO 3 sts. Knit 10 rows. Turn work 90° and pick up 5 sts along edge. Turn work 90° and pick up 3 sts from CO edge—11 sts total.

Set-up row (WS): K3, P5, K3.

Row 1 (RS): K2, YO, K1, M1, K1, PM, K3, PM, K1, M1, K1, YO, K2—15 sts.

Row 2: K2, YO, K1, purl to marker, SM, K3, SM, purl to last 3 sts, K1, YO, K2—17 sts.

Row 3: K2, YO, knit to 1 st before marker, M1, K1, SM, K3, SM, K1, M1, knit to last 2 sts, YO, K2—21 sts.

Rep rows 2 and 3 twice more—33 sts. Rep row 2 once more—35 sts.

BODY OF SHAWL

Work charts as follows.

Chart A—69 sts

Chart B—107 sts

Chart A—141 sts

Chart B—179 sts

Chart A—213 sts

Chart B—251 sts

Chart A—285 sts

Chart B—323 sts

Chart C—359 sts

Chart C—395 sts

Chart C—431 sts

Rows 1–6 only of chart C—449 sts

Make It Your Own!

It's easy to adjust the size of this shawl. Repeat charts A and B together (i.e., A, B, A, B, etc.) to the desired length, ending with chart B. Chart C can be repeated to desired length, ending with row 6. Want an even bigger shawl? Use a thicker yarn and the appropriate-sized needle for the yarn. Remember, when using a thicker yarn, you'll need additional yardage when following the pattern as written.

FINISHING

BO loosely kw (page 91). Block shawl to finished measurements given at beg of patt. With tapestry needle, weave in ends.

WRITTEN INSTRUCTIONS FOR CHARTS

If you prefer to follow row-by-row written instructions rather than a chart, use the following instructions.

Chart A

Row 1 (RS): K2, YO, *K1, P3, K5, P3; rep from * to 2 sts before marker, K1, M1, K1, SM, K3, SM, K1, M1, K1, *P3, K5, P3, K1; rep from * to last 2 sts, YO, K2.

Row 2 (WS): K2, YO, K1, *P1, K3, P5, K3; rep from * to 3 sts before marker, P3, SM, K3, SM, P3, *K3, P5, K3, P1; rep from * to last 3 sts, K1, YO, K2.

Row 3: K2, YO, K2, *K1, P2, K2, P1, K1, P1, K2, P2; rep from * to 3 sts before marker, K2, M1, K1, SM, K3, SM, K1, M1, K2, *P2, K2, P1, K1, P1, K2, P2, K1; rep from * to last 4 sts, K2, YO, K2.

Row 4: K2, YO, K1, P2, *P1, K2, P2, K1, P1, K1, P2, K2; rep from * to 4 sts before marker, P4, SM, K3, SM, P4, *K2, P2, K1, P1, K1, P2, K2, P1; rep from * to last 5 sts, P2, K1, YO, K2.

Row 5: K2, YO, K3, M1, K1, *K1, P1, K2, P2, K1, P2, K2, P1; rep from * to 4 sts before marker, K3, M1, K1, SM, K3, SM, K1, M1, K3, *P1, K2, P2, K1, P2, K2, P1, K1; rep from * to last 6 sts, K1, M1, K3, YO, K2.

Row 6: K2, YO, K1, P5, *P1, K1, P2, K2, P1, K2, P2, K1; rep from * to 5 sts before marker, P5, SM, K3, SM, P5, *K1, P2, K2, P1, K2, P2, K1, P1; rep from * to last 8 sts, P5, K1, YO, K2.

Row 7: K2, YO, K2, P3, K2, *K3, P3, K1, P3, K2; rep from * to 5 sts before marker, K4, M1, K1, SM, K3, SM, K1, M1, K4, *K2, P3, K1, P3, K3; rep from * to last 9 sts, K2, P3, K2, YO, K2.

Row 8: K2, YO, K1, P2, K3, P2, *P3, K3, P1, K3, P2; rep from * to 6 sts before marker, P6, SM, K3, SM, P6, *P2, K3, P1, K3, P3; rep from * to last 10 sts, P2, K3, P2, K1, YO, K2.

Row 9: K2, YO, K3, M1, K2, P3, K1, *K2, P3, K3, P3, K1; rep from * to 6 sts before marker, K5, M1, K1, SM, K3, SM, K1, M1, K5, *K1, P3, K3, P3, K2; rep from * to last 11 sts, K1, P3, K2, M1, K3, YO, K2.

The subtle chevron stitch pattern creates texture and makes the shawl reversible.

Row 10: K2, YO, K1, P6, K3, P1, *P2, K3, P3, K3, P1; rep from * to 7 sts before marker, P7, SM, K3, SM, P7, *P1, K3, P3, K3, P2; rep from * to last 13 sts, P1, K3, P6, K1, YO, K2.

Chart B

Row 1 (RS): K2, YO, *K1, P3, K5, P3; rep from * to 7 sts before marker, K1, P3, K2, M1, K1, SM, K3, SM, K1, M1, K2, P3, K1, *P3, K5, P3, K1; rep from * to last 2 sts, YO, K2.

Row 2 (WS): K2, YO, K1, *P1, K3, P5, K3; rep from * to 8 sts before marker, P1, K3, P4, SM, K3, SM, P4, K3, P1, *K3, P5, K3, P1; rep from * to last 3 sts, K1, YO, K2.

Row 3: K2, YO, K2, *K1, P2, K2, P1, K1, P1, K2, P2; rep from * to 8 sts before marker, K1, P2, K2, P1, K1, M1, K1, SM, K3, SM, K1, M1, K1, P1, K2, P2, K1, *P2, K2, P1, K1, P1, K2, P2, K1; rep from * to last 4 sts, K2, YO, K2.

Row 4: K2, YO, K1, P2, *P1, K2, P2, K1, P1, K1, P2, K2; rep from * to 9 sts before marker, P1, K2, P2, K1, P3, SM, K3, SM, P3, K1, P2, K2, P1, *K2, P2, K1, P1, K1, P2, K2, P1; rep from * to last 5 sts, P2, K1, YO, K2.

Row 5: K2, YO, K3, M1, K1, *K1, P1, K2, P2, K1, P2, K2, P1; rep from * to 9 sts before marker, K1, P1, K2, P2, K2, M1, K1, SM, K3, SM, K1, M1, K2, P2, K2, P1, K1, *P1, K2, P2, K1, P2, K2, P1, K1; rep from * to last 6 sts, K1, M1, K3, YO, K2.

Row 6: K2, YO, K1, P5, *P1, K1, P2, K2, P1, K2, P2, K1; rep from * to 10 sts before marker, P1, K1, P2, K2, P4, SM, K3, SM, P4, K2, P2, K1, P1, *K1, P2, K2, P1, K2, P2, K1, P1; rep from * to last 8 sts, P5, K1, YO, K2.

Row 7: K2, YO, K2, P3, K2, *K3, P3, K1, P3, K2; rep from * to 10 sts before marker, K3, P3, K1, M1, K2, M1, K1, SM, K3, SM, K1, M1, K2, M1, K1, P3, K3, *K2, P3, K1, P3, K3; rep from * to last 9 sts, K2, P3, K2, YO, K2.

Row 8: K2, YO, K1, P2, K3, P2, *P3, K3, P1, K3, P2; rep from * to 12 sts before marker, P3, K3, P6, SM, K3, SM, P6, K3, P3, *P2, K3, P1, K3, P3; rep from * to last 10 sts, P2, K3, P2, K1, YO, K2.

Row 9: K2, YO, K3, M1, K2, P3, K1, *K2, P3, K3, P3, K1; rep from * to 12 sts before marker, K2, P3, K4, M1, K2, M1, K1, SM, K3, SM, K1, M1, K2, M1, K4, P3, K2, *K1, P3, K3, P3, K2; rep from * to last 11 sts, K1, P3, K2, M1, K3, YO, K2.

Row 10: K2, YO, K1, P6, K3, P1, *P2, K3, P3, K3, P1; rep from * to 14 sts before marker, P2, K3, P9, SM, K3, SM, P9, K3, P2, *P1, K3, P3, K3, P2; rep from * to last 13 sts, P1, K3, P6, K1, YO, K2.

Chart C

Rows 1, 3, and 5 (RS): K2, YO, knit to 1 st before marker, M1, K1, SM, K3, SM, K1, M1, knit to the last 2 sts, YO, K2.

Rows 2, 4, and 6 (WS): K2, YO, knit to the last 2 sts, YO, K2.

Row 7: K2, YO, K1, P1, *K1 tbl, P1; rep from * to 1 st before marker, M1, K1, SM, K3, SM, K1, M1, *P1, K1 tbl; rep from * to last 4 sts, P1, K1, YO, K2.

Row 8: K2, YO, K1, *P1, K1; rep from * to 2 sts before marker, P2, SM, K3, SM, P2, *K1, P1; rep from * to last 3 sts, K1, YO, K2.

Row 9: K2, YO, K1, P1, *K1 tbl, P1; rep from * to 2 sts before marker, K1, M1, K1, SM, K3, SM, K1, M1, K1, *P1, K1 tbl; rep from * to last 4 sts, P1, K1, YO, K2.

Row 10: K2, YO, K1, *P1, K1; rep from * to 3 sts before marker, P3, SM, K3, SM, P3, *K1, P1; rep from * to last 3 sts, K1, YO, K2.

Row 11: K2, YO, K1, P1, *K1 tbl, P1; rep from * to 3 sts before marker, K2, M1, K1, SM, K3, SM, K1, M1, K2, *P1, K1 tbl; rep from * to last 4 sts, P1, K1, YO, K2.

Row 12: K2, YO, K1, *P1, K1; rep from * to 4 sts before marker, P4, SM, K3, SM, P4, *K1, P1; rep from * to last 3 sts, K1, YO, K2.

Rep rows 1–12 for patt.

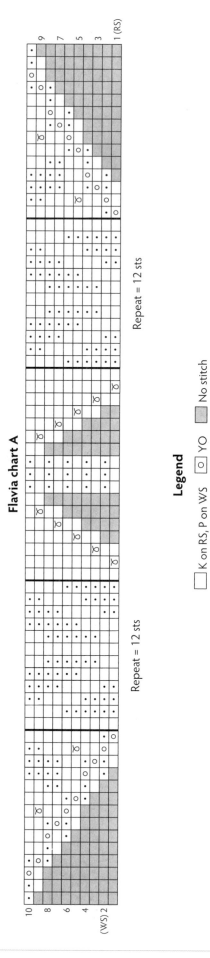

Flavia chart A

Repeat = 12 sts

Repeat = 12 sts

Legend

☐ K on RS, P on WS

· P on RS, K on WS

☐ No stitch

○ YO

☒ M1

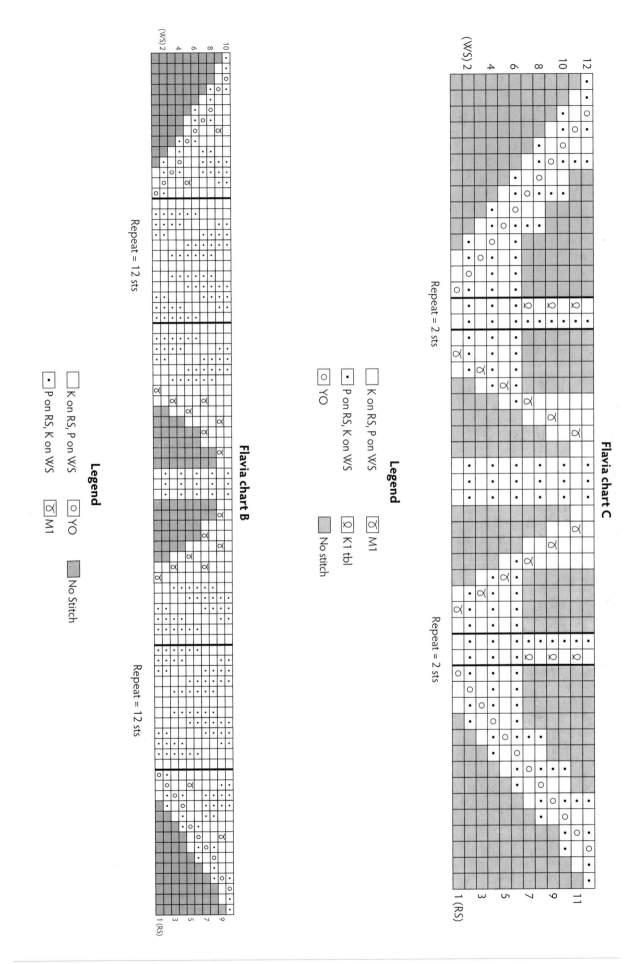

Flavia chart C

Repeat = 2 sts

Repeat = 2 sts

Legend

☐ K on RS, P on WS

• P on RS, K on WS

⊙ YO

☒ M1

Ω K1 tbl

▨ No stitch

Flavia chart B

Repeat = 12 sts

Legend

☐ K on RS, P on WS

• P on RS, K on WS

⊙ YO

☒ M1

▨ No Stitch

DAMSEL

Designed and knit by author

A lace pattern used two ways makes for an interesting project. This shawl is worked from the top down using an allover lace pattern; a knitted-on border is added at the end using the same motif with a slight variation.

SKILL LEVEL: Intermediate

FINISHED MEASUREMENTS:
70" x 23"

MATERIALS

3 skeins of Tosh DK from
   Madelinetosh (100%
   superwash merino wool;
   100 g; 225 yards) in color
   Gossamer **3**
US size 6 (4.0 mm) circular
   needle, 32" cable or longer,
   or size required for gauge
Tapestry needle
Blocking supplies

GAUGE

20 sts and 28 rows = 4" in St st

Gauge is not critical in this patt, but a different gauge will affect yardage and size of shawl.

PATTERN NOTES

Charts are on pages 15 and 16. If you prefer to follow written instructions for the charted material, see "Written Instructions for Charts" on page 14.

For chart B, the final ssk on RS rows is worked by using last st from border and first st on LH needle from body of shawl.

On row 7 of chart B, after binding off 3 sts, there is 1 st on RH needle, this counts as the first st worked after the stitches are bound off (i.e., it's the first st of the K4 that follows the binding off).

INSTRUCTIONS

Work garter-tab CO (page 90) as follows:

CO 2 sts. Knit 22 rows. Turn work 90° and pick up 11 sts along edge. Turn work 90° and pick up 2 sts from CO edge—15 sts total.

Set-up row (WS): K2, P11, K2.

Inc row (RS): K2, (YO, K1) to last 2 sts, YO, K2—27 sts.

Next row: K2, purl to last 2 sts, K2.

BODY OF SHAWL

Work rows 1–8 of chart A 11 times total. Work rows 1–7 of chart A once more.

STITCH COUNT FOR BODY OF SHAWL	
Rep 1 of chart A	51 sts
Rep 2 of chart A	75 sts
Rep 3 of chart A	99 sts
Rep 4 of chart A	123 sts
Rep 5 of chart A	147 sts
Rep 6 of chart A	171 sts
Rep 7 of chart A	195 sts
Rep 8 of chart A	219 sts
Rep 9 of chart A	243 sts
Rep 10 of chart A	267 sts
Rep 11 of chart A	291 sts
Rows 1–7 of chart A	313 sts

Make It Your Own!

It's easy to adjust the size of this shawl, making it a great project for substituting yarn weights. Work chart A to the desired length, and then work rows 1–7 of chart A once more. Finish the body of the shawl by working the final wrong-side row. Work the lace border section as written, adjusting the number of times chart B is worked as necessary. Remember, changing the size of the shawl and the yarn weight will affect the amount of yarn needed to complete the piece.

Next row (WS): K2, YO, (K1, K1f&b) twice, knit to the last 4 sts, K1f&b, K1, YO, K2—318 sts.

Lace Border

Using knitted CO (page 90), CO 17 sts.

Next row (RS): K16, ssk with 1 st from body of shawl.

Next row (WS): Sl 1 wyib, knit to end.

Work chart B 79 times.

Next row (RS): K16, ssk with 1 st from body of shawl.

Next row (WS): Sl 1 wyib, knit to end.

FINISHING

BO loosely kw (page 91). Block shawl to finished measurements given at beg of patt. With tapestry needle, weave in ends.

WRITTEN INSTRUCTIONS FOR CHARTS

If you prefer to follow row-by-row written instructions rather than a chart, use the following instructions.

Chart A

Row 1 (RS): K2, (YO, K1) twice, *K2tog, (K1, YO) twice, K1, ssk, K5; rep from * to last 11 sts, K2tog, (K1, YO) twice, K1, ssk, (K1, YO) twice, K2.

Row 2 and all even-numbered rows (WS): K2, YO, K1, purl to the last 3 sts, K1, YO, K2.

Row 3: K2, YO, K1, YO, K3, K2tog, *K1, YO, K3, YO, K1, sssk, (K1, YO, K1) into next st, K3tog; rep from * to last 13 sts, K1, YO, K3, YO, K1, ssk, K3, YO, K1, YO, K2.

Row 5: K2, (YO, K1) twice, K2tog, (K1, YO) twice, K1, *ssk, K5, K2tog, (K1, YO) twice, K1; rep from * to last 6 sts, ssk, (K1, YO) twice, K2.

Row 7: K2, YO, K1, YO, K3, K2tog, K1, YO, K3, YO, *K1, sssk, (K1, YO, K1) into next st, K3tog, K1, YO, K3, YO; rep from * to last 9 sts, K1, ssk, K3, YO, K1, YO, K2.

Row 8: K2, YO, K1, purl to the last 3 sts, K1, YO, K2.

Rep rows 1–8 for patt.

Chart B

Row 1 (RS): K2, YO, K2tog, YO, K1, K2tog, (K1, YO) twice, K1, ssk, K4, ssk the last border st with the first body st on left needle.

Row 2 and all even-numbered rows (WS): Sl 1 wyib, K1, purl to the last 2 sts, K2.

Row 3: K2, YO, K2tog, YO, K1, K2tog, K1, YO, K3, YO, K1, ssk, K3, ssk the last border st with the first body st on left needle.

Row 5: K2, YO, K2tog, (YO, K1) twice, ssk, K5, K2tog, K1, YO, K2, ssk the last border st with the first body st on left needle.

Row 7: BO 3 sts, K4, YO, K1, sssk, (K1, YO, K1) into next st, K3tog, K1, YO, K3, ssk the last border st with the first body st on left needle.

Row 8: Sl 1 wyib, K1, purl to the last 2 sts, K2.

Rep rows 1–8 for patt.

Legend

☐ K on RS, P on WS	人 K3tog on RS
• P on RS, K on WS	人 Sssk on RS
O YO	✕ (K1, YO, K1) into same st
╲ K2tog on RS	▨ No stitch
╱ Ssk on RS	

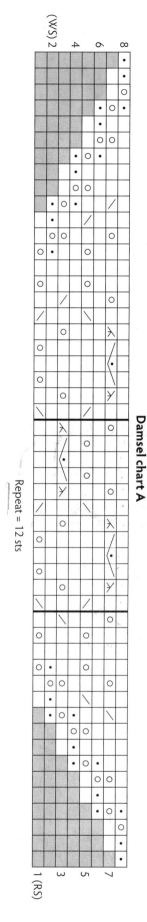

Damsel chart A

Repeat = 12 sts

The body of this shawl contains an allover stitch pattern. The same stitch is slightly modified and used in the lace border edging.

Damsel chart B

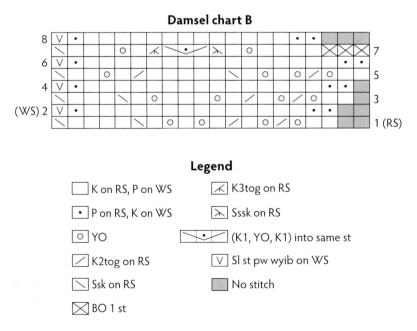

Legend

☐ K on RS, P on WS	⬉ K3tog on RS
• P on RS, K on WS	⬊ Sssk on RS
○ YO	⟋•⟍ (K1, YO, K1) into same st
╱ K2tog on RS	V Sl st pw wyib on WS
╲ Ssk on RS	▨ No stitch
⊠ BO 1 st	

LARI

Designed and knit by author

This is a simple cowl or infinity scarf with the volume turned up. An increasing lace panel is inserted into a background of stockinette stitch, adding interest and beauty to the project—and your wardrobe!

SKILL LEVEL: Intermediate

SIZES: Cowl (Infinity Scarf)

FINISHED CIRCUMFERENCE:
24 (48)" slightly stretched

FINISHED DEPTH: 6½"

MATERIALS

1 skein of Lively DK from Hazel Knits (90% superwash merino, 10% nylon; 130 g; 275 yards) in color Tropical Sunset 3
US size 6 (4.0 mm) circular needle, 16 (32)" cable or longer, or size required for gauge
3 stitch markers
Tapestry needle
Blocking supplies

GAUGE

20 sts and 32 rows = 4" in St st

Gauge is not critical in this patt, but a different gauge will affect yardage and size of cowl.

PATTERN NOTES

Chart is on page 20. If you prefer to follow written instructions for the charted material, see "Written Instructions for Chart" on page 20.

The pattern is written for the cowl with the instructions for the infinity scarf written in

parentheses ( ), where necessary. If only one instruction is given, it should be worked for both sizes. The infinity scarf is shown.

For this project, three stitch markers are used. You may find it helpful to use two matching markers for the chart and a different stitch marker to mark the beginning of the round.

INSTRUCTIONS

CO 100 (200) sts. Join in the round, being careful not to twist sts. PM to mark beg of rnd.

Ribbing rnd: *K1, P1; rep from * to end of rnd.

Rep ribbing rnd another 4 times (5 rnds total).

Set-up rnd: K2, M1, K43 (93), PM, K9, PM, knit to end of rnd—101 (201) sts.

Rnd 1: Knit to 2 sts before the marker, K2tog, SM, work row 1 of chart to next marker, SM, ssk, knit to end of rnd.

Rnd 2: Knit to marker, SM, work row 2 of chart to marker, SM, knit to end of rnd.

Rnd 3: Knit to 2 sts before marker, K2tog, SM, work next row of chart to marker, SM, ssk, knit to end of rnd.

Rnd 4: Knit to marker, SM, work next row of chart to marker, SM, knit to end of rnd.

Rep rnds 3 and 4 another 21 times, working next subsequent rnd of chart each rnd—55 sts total in between markers for chart.

An increasing lace panel adds a captivating detail to this otherwise simple project.

Make It Your Own!

Want a wider cowl? Keep repeating rounds 3 and 4, working the next subsequent round of the chart to your desired length, ending with round 6 or 14. Work the remainder of the pattern as written. Adding rounds to your cowl or infinity scarf will increase the amount of yarn needed to complete the project.

Next rnd: K2, K2tog, knit to marker, remove marker, knit to next marker, remove marker, knit to end of rnd—100 (200) sts.

Work ribbing rnd for 5 rnds.

FINISHING

BO loosely in patt. Block cowl to finished measurements given at beg of patt. With tapestry needle, weave in ends.

The infinity scarf can be doubled around the neck for extra warmth.

WRITTEN INSTRUCTIONS FOR CHART

If you prefer to follow row-by-row written instructions rather than a chart, use the following instructions.

Rnds 1, 3, and 5: YO, knit to marker, YO.

Rnds 2, 4, and 6: Knit all sts.

Rnd 7: YO, K3, *K2, K2tog, YO, K1, YO, ssk, K1; rep from * to 4 sts before marker, K4, YO.

Rnd 8: K4, *K1, K2tog, YO, K3, YO, ssk; rep from * to 5 sts before marker, K5.

Rnds 9, 11, and 13: YO, knit to marker, YO.

Rnds 10, 12, and 14: Knit all sts.

Rnd 15: YO, K1, K2tog, YO, K1, YO, ssk, K1, *K2, K2tog, YO, K1, YO, ssk, K1; rep from * to marker, YO.

Rnd 16: *K1, K2tog, YO, K3, YO, ssk; rep from * to 1 st before marker, K1.

Rep rows 1–16 for patt.

Lari chart

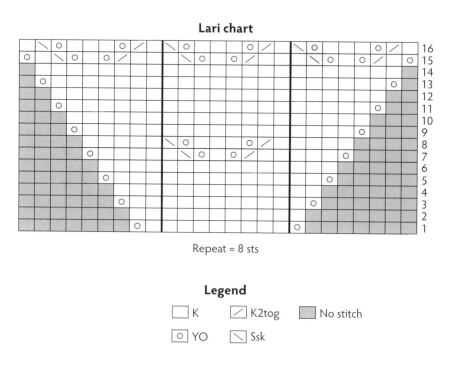

Repeat = 8 sts

Legend

☐ K	╱ K2tog	▨ No stitch	
○ YO	╲ Ssk		

MEDLEY

Designed by author and knit by Jenni Lesniak

There's something I love about simple ribbed scarves, but the unfortunate truth is that they can be a bit boring to knit. Not this scarf! Small cables are inserted between alternating rib patterns, making this scarf both fun to knit and cozy to wear.

SKILL LEVEL: Easy

FINISHED MEASUREMENTS:
9½" x 70"

MATERIALS

4 skeins of City Tweed DK from Knit Picks (55% merino wool, 25% superfine alpaca, 20% Donegal tweed; 50 g; 123 yards) in color Blue Blood **3**

US size 7 (4.5 mm) knitting needles, or size required for gauge

Cable needle
Tapestry needle
Blocking supplies

GAUGE

18 sts and 28 rows = 4" in K2, P2 ribbing, stretched

Gauge is not critical in this patt, but a different gauge will affect yardage and size of scarf.

PATTERN NOTES

Chart is on page 23. If you prefer to follow written instructions for the charted material, see "Written Instructions for Chart" on page 23.

This scarf is worked primarily in a ribbed pattern. You may find it helpful to use a stitch marker to mark the right side of your project.

SPECIAL ABBREVIATION

1/1 RC: Slip 1 st to cable needle, hold in back, K1, K1 from cable needle

Make It Your Own!

Medley is very easy to modify. You can change up the width of the scarf simply by casting on any multiple of 4 + 2 stitches. Because the cast-on number is so easy to change, this is another great project to use a different yarn weight if you want. Use the appropriate needle for your yarn, decide how many stitches to cast on, and get knitting. Remember, changing the stitch count and/or yarn weight will affect how much yarn you need to complete your scarf.

INSTRUCTIONS

CO 42 sts.

Work chart until scarf measures approx 70", ending with row 8 or 18 of chart.

FINISHING

BO loosely in patt. Block scarf to finished measurements given at beg of patt. With tapestry needle, weave in ends.

WRITTEN INSTRUCTIONS FOR CHART

If you prefer to follow row-by-row written instructions rather than a chart, use the following instructions.

Row 1 (RS): *K2, P2; rep from * to last 2 sts, K2.

Row 2 (WS): P2, *K2, P2; rep from * to end.

Rows 3–8: Rep rows 1 and 2.

Row 9: *1/1 RC; rep from * to end.

Row 10: K2, *P2, K2; rep from * to end.

Row 11: *P2, K2; rep from * to last 2 sts, P2.

Rows 12–17: Rep rows 10 and 11.

Row 18: Rep row 10.

Row 19: *1/1 RC; rep from * to end.

Row 20: Rep row 2.

Rep rows 1–20 for patt.

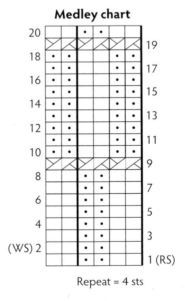

Medley chart

Repeat = 4 sts

Legend

☐ K on RS, P on WS

• P on RS, K on WS

⧖ 1/1 RC

With the staggered ribbing and cables worked all the way across a row, even the reverse side of this project looks great. The top photo shows the front of the scarf; the bottom shows the reverse.

CHEYENNE

Designed by author and knit by Cathy Rusk

I can't help myself—I love combining garter stitch and lace. Cheyenne uses simple triangle-lace patterns broken up by rows of garter stitch with semicircular shaping.

SKILL LEVEL: Intermediate

FINISHED MEASUREMENTS:
54" x 26"

MATERIALS

3 skeins of Cricket from Anzula Luxury Fibers (80% superwash merino, 10% cashmere, 10% nylon; 100 g; 250 yards) in color Coco **3**

US size 6 (4.0 mm) circular needle, 32" cable or longer, or size required for gauge
Tapestry needle
Blocking supplies

GAUGE

20 sts and 28 rows = 4" in St st

Gauge is not critical in this patt, but a different gauge will affect yardage and size of shawl.

PATTERN NOTES

Charts are on pages 26 and 27. If you prefer to follow written instructions for the charted material, see "Written Instructions for Charts" on page 26.

INSTRUCTIONS

Work garter-tab CO (page 90) as follows:

CO 2 sts. Knit 20 rows. Turn work 90° and pick up 10 sts along edge. Turn work 90° and pick up 2 sts from CO edge—14 sts total.

Set-up row (WS): Knit all sts.

Row 1 (RS): K2, (YO, K1) to the last 2 sts, YO, K2—25 sts.

Row 2: K2, purl to the last 2 sts, K2.

Row 3: Knit all sts.

Row 4: Rep row 2.

BODY OF SHAWL

Inc row (RS): K2, (K1, YO) to the last 3 sts, K3—45 sts.

Row 1 (WS): K2, purl to the last 2 sts, K2.

Row 2: Knit all sts.

Rep rows 1 and 2 another 3 times. Rep row 1 once more.

Work inc row—85 sts.

Next row: Rep row 1.

Work chart A once (14 rows).

Work inc row—165 sts.

Next row: Rep row 1.

Work chart A twice (28 rows).

Work inc row—325 sts.

Next row: Rep row 1.

Work chart B twice (28 rows).

Work chart C twice (28 rows).

Work in garter st (knit every row) for 6 rows, ending with a WS row.

FINISHING

BO loosely kw (page 91) on RS. Block shawl to finished measurements given at beg of patt. With tapestry needle, weave in ends.

WRITTEN INSTRUCTIONS FOR CHARTS

If you prefer to follow row-by-row written instructions rather than a chart, use the following instructions.

Make It Your Own!

The charts for this pattern are all interchangeable. If you love one chart, you can use it in place of another one in the pattern. You can also add additional repeats of chart C before working the last six rows of garter stitch. If you want a giant snuggly shawl, you can easily modify this pattern to get one. Work as written, until chart C has been completed twice. Work another increase row to give a new stitch count of 645 sts. Work eight chart repeats of whatever chart you like. Finish off with the six rows of garter stitch and bind off. Remember, working extra chart repeats means you will need additional yarn.

Chart A

Rows 1–7: Knit all sts.

Rows 8, 10, and 12 (WS): K2, purl to the last 2 sts, K2.

Row 9 (RS): K2, *K1, YO, ssk, K3, K2tog, YO; rep from * to last 3 sts, K3.

Row 11: K2, *K2, YO, ssk, K1, K2tog, YO, K1; rep from * to last 3 sts, K3.

Row 13: K2, *K3, YO, CDD, YO, K2; rep from * to last 3 sts, K3.

Row 14: K2, purl to the last 2 sts, K2.

Rep rows 1–14 for patt.

Cheyenne chart A

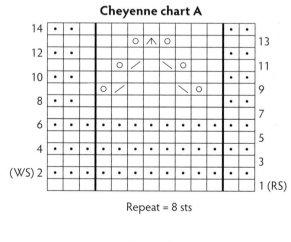

Repeat = 8 sts

Legend

	K on RS, P on WS		K2tog
•	P on RS, K on WS		Ssk
o	YO		CDD

Chart B

Rows 1–7: Knit all sts.

Rows 8, 10, and 12 (WS): K2, purl to the last 2 sts, K2.

Row 9 (RS): K2, *K1, YO, K2, CDD, K2, YO; rep from * to last 3 sts, K3.

Row 11: K2, *K2, YO, K1, CDD, K1, YO, K1; rep from * to last 3 sts, K3.

Row 13: K2, *K3, YO, CDD, YO, K2; rep from * to last 3 sts, K3.

Row 14: K2, purl to the last 2 sts, K2.

Rep rows 1–14 for patt.

Chart C

Rows 1–7: Knit all sts.

Rows 8, 10, and 12 (WS): K2, purl to the last 2 sts, K2.

Row 9 (RS): K2, *K1, YO, K2, CDD, K2, YO; rep from * to last 3 sts, K3.

Row 11: K2, *YO, ssk, YO, K1, CDD, K1, YO, K1; rep from * to last 3 sts, K3.

Row 13: K2, *K1, YO, ssk, YO, CDD, YO, K2tog, YO; rep from * to last 3 sts, K3.

Row 14: K2, purl to the last 2 sts, K2.

Rep rows 1–14 for patt.

Semicircular shawl shaping, garter stitch, and lace are the perfect combination for a cozy shawl!

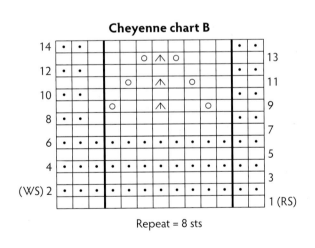

Cheyenne chart B

Repeat = 8 sts

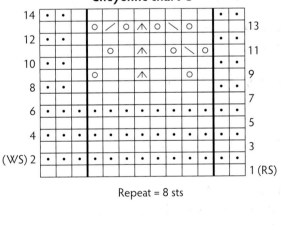

Cheyenne chart C

Repeat = 8 sts

Legend

☐ K on RS, P on WS

• P on RS, K on WS

○ YO

⋀ CDD

Legend

☐ K on RS, P on WS   ╱ K2tog

• P on RS, K on WS   ╲ Ssk

○ YO   ⋀ CDD

NORFOLK

Designed and knit by author

I can spend hours reading about fisherman sweaters and looking at photos of them. I plan to make one someday, but in the meantime, this cute hat using a traditional stitch pattern will have to do!

SKILL LEVEL: Intermediate

SIZES: Adult Small (Adult Large)

FINISHED CIRCUMFERENCE: 18", fits up to 20" (21", fits up to 23")

FINISHED LENGTH: 8½ (10)"

MATERIALS

1 skein of Vintage DK from Berroco (52% acrylic, 40% wool, 8% nylon; 100 g; 290 yards) in color Cerulean 21190 **3**

US size 6 (4.0 mm) circular needle, 16" cable, or size required for gauge

Set of 5 double-pointed needles in US size 6 (4.0 mm) or size required for gauge

1 stitch marker

Tapestry needle

GAUGE

24 sts and 28 rows = 4" in St st

PATTERN NOTES

Chart is on page 30. If you prefer to follow written instructions for the charted material, see "Written Instructions for Chart" on page 30.

The pattern is written for the Adult Small with the instructions for Adult Large written in parentheses ( ), where necessary. If only one instruction is given, it should be worked for both sizes. The Adult Small is shown.

The charming diamond motif on this hat is created by a simple knit-and-purl stitch pattern.

INSTRUCTIONS

With circular needle, CO 96 (112) sts. Join in the round, being careful not to twist sts. PM to mark start of rnd.

Ribbing rnd: *K2, P2; rep from * to end of rnd.

Work ribbing rnd for another 11 (15) rnds.

Work 4 rnds of St st (knit every rnd). Work chart one time (16 rnds). Cont working in St st until hat measures 6½ (7½)" from CO edge. Dec as follows.

Note: Switch to dpns when stitches no longer comfortably fit on 16" circular.

Rnd 1: *K6, K2tog; rep from * to end of rnd—84 (98) sts.

Rnds 2, 4, 6, 8, and 10: Knit all sts.

Rnd 3: *K5, K2tog; rep from * to end of rnd—72 (84) sts.

Rnd 5: *K4, K2tog; rep from * to end of rnd—60 (70) sts.

Rnd 7: *K3, K2tog; rep from * to end of rnd—48 (56) sts.

Rnd 9: *K2, K2tog; rep from * to end of rnd—36 (42) sts.

Rnd 11: *K1, K2tog; rep from * to end of rnd—24 (28) sts.

Rnd 12: *K2tog; rep from * to end of rnd—12 (14) sts.

FINISHING

Cut yarn, leaving 8" tail. Thread yarn onto tapestry needle and thread through rem sts. Gather sts and tie off. Weave in ends.

WRITTEN INSTRUCTIONS FOR CHART

If you prefer to follow row-by-row written instructions rather than a chart, use the following instructions.

Rnds 1 and 2: *K6, P2, K8; rep from * to end of rnd.

Rnds 3 and 4: *K4, P2, K2, P2, K6; rep from * to end of rnd.

Rnds 5 and 6: *(K2, P2) 3 times, K4; rep from * to end of rnd.

Rnds 7 and 8: *P2, K2; rep from * to end of rnd.

Rnds 9 and 10: Rep rnds 5 and 6.

Rnds 11 and 12: Rep rnds 3 and 4.

Rnds 13 and 14: Rep rnds 1 and 2.

Norfolk chart

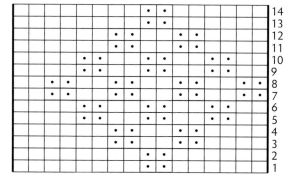

Repeat = 16 sts

Legend

☐ K

⊡ P

MALMESBURY

Designed and knit by author

There are times when you want to keep your ears warm, but you don't want to wear a hat. This lightweight headband is the perfect solution. It's such a quick project that your ears will be safe from the cold in no time!

SKILL LEVEL: Intermediate

FINISHED MEASUREMENTS:
5" x 20" (stretches up to 22")

MATERIALS

1 skein of Merino DK from String Theory Hand Dyed Yarns (100% superwash merino wool; 113 g; 280 yards) in color Avalon ⟨3⟩
US size 5 (3.75 mm) knitting needles, or size required for gauge
Tapestry needle
Blocking supplies
1 button, 1" diameter

GAUGE

20 sts and 21 rows = 4" in St st

PATTERN NOTES

Charts are on page 34. If you prefer to follow written instructions for the charted material, see "Written Instructions for Charts" on page 33.

Headband is written for one size and will stretch to fit a variety of heads. To adjust size, work chart B as written until the piece is 3" shorter than desired length, ending with row 8. Work remainder of pattern as written.

INSTRUCTIONS

CO 5 sts.

Beginning Button Band

Knit 3 rows.

Row 1 (RS): K2, M1L, knit to the last 2 sts, M1R, K2—7 sts.

Rows 2, 4, and 6 (WS): Knit all sts.

Row 3: K2, M1L, K1, YO, K2tog, M1R, K2—9 sts.

Row 5: Rep row 1—11 sts.

Row 7: Rep row 1—13 sts.

Row 8: Knit all sts.

Lace

Work chart A—21 sts. Work rows 1–8 of chart B until headband measures 16" from CO edge, ending with row 8. Work chart C once—13 sts.

Final Button Band

Row 1 (RS): K2, ssk, knit to the last 4 sts, K2tog, K2—11 sts.

Rows 2, 4, and 6 (WS): Knit all sts.

Row 3: Rep row 1—9 sts.

Row 5: Rep row 1—7 sts.

Row 7: K1, ssk, K1, K2tog, K1—5 sts.

Knit 3 rows.

FINISHING

BO loosely kw (page 91) on RS. Block piece to dimensions given at beg of patt. With tapestry needle, weave in ends. Sew button on button band to match up with corresponding buttonhole.

WRITTEN INSTRUCTIONS FOR CHARTS

If you prefer to follow row-by-row written instructions rather than a chart, use the following instructions.

A single button holds the headband together.

Chart A

Row 1 (RS): K2, M1L, K1, YO, K2, CDD, K2, YO, K1, M1R, K2.

Rows 2, 4, and 6 (WS): K2, purl to the last 2 sts, K2.

Row 3: K2, M1L, K1, YO, K3, CDD, K3, YO, K1, M1R, K2.

Row 5: K2, M1L, K1, YO, K4, CDD, K4, YO, K1, M1R, K2.

Row 7: K2, M1L, K1, YO, K5, CDD, K5, YO, K1, M1R, K2.

Row 8: Knit all sts.

Chart B

Row 1 (RS): K3, (YO, ssk) 3 times, YO, CDD, (YO, K2tog) 3 times, YO, K3.

Rows 2, 4, and 6 (WS): K2, purl to the last 2 sts, K2.

Rows 3, 5, and 7: K3, YO, K6, CDD, K6, YO, K3.

Row 8: Knit all sts.

Rep rows 1–8 for patt.

Chart C

Row 1 (RS): K2, ssk, YO, K5, CDD, K5, YO, K2tog, K2.

Rows 2, 4, 6, and 8 (WS): K2, purl to the last 2 sts, K2.

Row 3: K2, ssk, YO, K4, CDD, K4, YO, K2tog, K2.

Row 5: K2, ssk, YO, K3, CDD, K3, YO, K2tog, K2.

Row 7: K2, ssk, YO, K2, CDD, K2, YO, K2tog, K2.

Malmesbury chart A

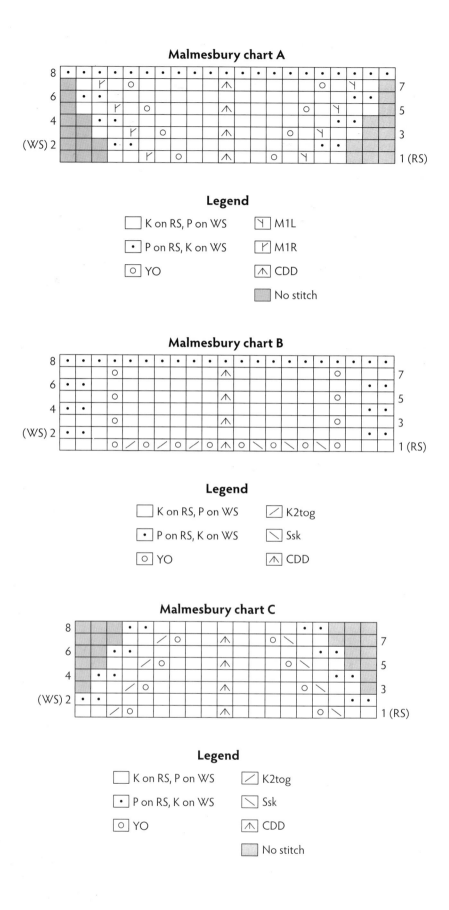

Legend

☐	K on RS, P on WS	⅄	M1L
•	P on RS, K on WS	⅄	M1R
○	YO	⋏	CDD
▦	No stitch		

Malmesbury chart B

Legend

☐	K on RS, P on WS	╱	K2tog
•	P on RS, K on WS	╲	Ssk
○	YO	⋏	CDD

Malmesbury chart C

Legend

☐	K on RS, P on WS	╱	K2tog
•	P on RS, K on WS	╲	Ssk
○	YO	⋏	CDD
▦	No stitch		

MEROPE

Designed by author and knit by Jenni Lesniak

Slipped-stitch cables are perfect for the slightly variegated yarn in this project. These fingerless mitts are worked as mirror images of each other, keeping the knitting interesting so you'll have no problem starting (and finishing) the second one!

SKILL LEVEL: Intermediate

FINISHED CIRCUMFERENCE: 7", fits up to 9"

FINISHED LENGTH: 12"

MATERIALS

1 skein of Core DK from Fiberstory (100% superwash merino; 100 g; 231 yards) in color Nymph

Set of 5 double-pointed needles in US size 6 (4.0 mm) or size required for gauge
2 stitch markers

Cable needle
Stitch holder or waste yarn
Tapestry needle
Blocking supplies

GAUGE

20 sts and 32 rows = 4" in K3, P2 ribbing, slightly stretched

PATTERN NOTES

Charts are on page 37. If you prefer to follow written instructions for the charted material, see "Written Instructions for Charts" on page 37.

The mitts are mirror images of each other, so be sure to use the correct chart when knitting each mitt!

SPECIAL ABBREVIATIONS

1/2 LC: Sl 1 st to cn, hold in front, K2, K1 from cn

1/2 RC: Sl 2 sts to cn, hold in back, K1, K2 from cn

RIGHT MITT

CO 50 sts. Divide stitches evenly on 4 dpns. Join in the round, being careful not to twist sts. PM to mark beg of rnd.

Ribbing rnd: *K3, P2; rep from * to end of rnd.

Rep ribbing rnd for 11 more rnds (12 rnds total).

Working right mitt chart patt 10 times on each rnd, work chart 4 times (48 rnds total).

Thumb Gusset

Rnd 1: Work rnd 1 of right mitt chart to end of rnd, PM, M1—51 sts.

Rnd 2: Work rnd 2 of right mitt chart to marker, SM, K1.

Rnd 3: Work next rnd of right mitt chart to marker, SM, M1, knit to end, M1—53 sts.

Rnd 4: Work next rnd of right mitt chart to marker, SM, knit to end.

Cont working in patt for right mitt chart on subsequent rows (starting with rnd 5), rep rnds 3 and 4 another 2 times—61 sts; 50 sts for hand and 11 sts for thumb.

Hand

Next rnd: Work next rnd of right mitt chart to marker, remove marker, place 11 sts on holder or waste yarn.

Work in established right mitt chart patt for another 11 rnds. Work ribbing rnd for 6 rnds. BO loosely in patt.

Thumb

Carefully transfer held sts from holder to dpns. Place 6 sts on needle 1, 5 sts on needle 2. With needle 3, pick up 4 sts in gap where thumb meets

hand—15 sts total. Redistribute sts to 5 sts on each needle.

Rnds 1–3: Knit all sts.

Rnds 4–6: (K3, P2) to end.

BO loosely in patt.

LEFT MITT

Using left mitt chart, work left mitt same as right mitt.

WRITTEN INSTRUCTIONS FOR CHARTS

If you prefer to follow row-by-row written instructions rather than a chart, use the following instructions.

Right Mitt Chart

Rnds 1 and 2: *K3, P2; rep from * to end of rnd.

Rnds 3 and 4: *Sl 1, K2, P2; rep from * to end of rnd.

Rnd 5: *1/2 LC, P2; rep from * to end of rnd.

Rnd 6: Rep rnd 1.

Rnds 7 and 8: *P2, K3; rep from * to end of rnd.

Rnds 9 and 10: *P2, sl 1, K2; rep from * to end of rnd.

Rnd 11: *P2, 1/2 LC; rep from * to end of rnd.

Rnd 12: Rep rnd 7.

Rep rnds 1–12 for patt.

Left Mitt Chart

Rnds 1 and 2: *K3, P2; rep from * to end of rnd.

Rnds 3 and 4: *K2, sl 1, P2; rep from * to end of rnd.

Rnd 5: *1/2 RC, P2; rep from * to end of rnd.

Rnd 6: Rep rnd 1.

Rnds 7 and 8: *P2, K3; rep from * to end of rnd.

Rnds 9 and 10: *P2, K2, sl 1; rep from * to end of rnd.

Rnd 11: *P2, 1/2 RC; rep from * to end of rnd.

Rnd 12: Rep rnd 7.

Rep rnds 1–12 for patt.

Merope right mitt chart

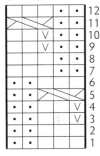

Repeat = 5 sts

Legend

☐ K on RS, P on WS

• P on RS, K on WS

V Sl 1 pw wyib

1/2 LC

Merope left mitt chart

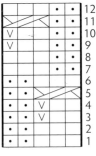

Repeat = 5 sts

Legend

☐ K   V Sl 1 pw wyib

• P   1/2 RC

ASTILBE

Designed and knit by author

These mitts take feather and fan to another level. With extreme decreases on each side of the lace panel, dramatic shape and texture are created in the lace pattern.

SKILL LEVEL: Intermediate

FINISHED CIRCUMFERENCE: 6½", fits up to 8½"

FINISHED LENGTH: 7½"

MATERIALS

1 skein of Extra from Blue Sky Alpacas (50% baby alpaca, 50% fine merino; 150 g; 218 yards) in color Shale **4**
Set of 5 double-pointed needles in US size 7 (4.5 mm) or size required for gauge
2 stitch markers
Stitch holder or waste yarn
Tapestry needle

GAUGE

20 sts and 24 rows = 4" in St st

PATTERN NOTES

Chart is on page 41. If you prefer to follow written instructions for the charted material, see "Written Instructions for Chart" on page 41.

Be sure to use "left mitt" and "right mitt" instructions, when necessary. If no left/right indication is given, work the same for both mitts.

BEGINNING RIBBING (BOTH MITTS)

CO 34 sts. Divide stitches evenly on 4 dpns. Join in the round, being careful not to twist sts. PM to mark beg of rnd.

Ribbing rnd: [(K1, P1) 8 times, K1] twice.

Rep ribbing rnd for 9 more rnds (10 rnds total).

LEFT MITT

Rnd 1: Work rnd 1 of chart over next 17 sts, knit to end.

Rnd 2: Work rnd 2 of chart over next 17 sts, knit to end.

Simple stockinette stitch is worked on the palms of the mitts.

Rnd 3: Work rnd 3 of chart over next 17 sts, knit to end.

Rnd 4: Work rnd 4 of chart over next 17 sts, knit to end.

Work rnds 1–4 another 6 times (7 times/28 rnds total).

Thumb Gusset

Rnd 1: Work rnd 1 of chart over next 17 sts, knit to end, PM, M1, PM—35 sts.

Rnd 2: Work rnd 2 of chart over next 17 sts, knit to marker, SM, K1.

Rnd 3: Work rnd 3 of chart over next 17 sts, knit to marker, SM, M1, knit to end, M1—37 sts.

Rnd 4: Work rnd 4 of chart over next 17 sts, knit to marker, SM, knit to end.

Working 4 Stitches at Once

Having trouble with K4tog and ssssk? Try this instead:

For K4tog: K2tog twice, slip the 2 stitches just made back to left-hand needle, pass the second stitch from the end over the first stitch. Slip that stitch back to the right-hand needle and continue working pattern.

For ssssk: K2tog twice, pass the second stitch on the right-hand needle over the first stitch and continue working pattern.

Working these stitches this way will change the look of the lace slightly—but they are much easier to work!

Rnd 5: Work rnd 1 of chart over next 17 sts, knit to marker, SM, M1, knit to end, M1—39 sts.

Rnd 6: Work rnd 2 of chart over next 17 sts, knit to marker, SM, knit to end.

Rep rnds 3–6 twice more—47 sts; 34 sts for hand and 13 sts for thumb. Rep rnds 3 and 4 once more—49 sts; 34 sts for hand and 15 sts for thumb.

Hand

Next rnd: Work rnd 1 of chart over next 17 sts, knit to marker, remove marker, place 15 sts on holder or waste yarn.

Work in established patt for another 3 rnds. Work ribbing rnd for 6 rnds. BO loosely in patt.

RIGHT MITT

Rnd 1: K17, work rnd 1 of chart to end.

Rnd 2: K17, work rnd 2 of chart to end.

Rnd 3: K17, work rnd 3 of chart to end.

Rnd 4: K17, work rnd 4 of chart to end.

Work rnds 1–4 another 6 times (7 times/28 rnds total).

Thumb Gusset

Rnd 1: K17, work rnd 1 of chart over next 17 sts to end, PM, M1, PM—35 sts.

Rnd 2: K17, work rnd 2 of chart over next 17 sts to marker, SM, K1.

Rnd 3: K17, work rnd 3 of chart over next 17 sts to marker, SM, M1, knit to end, M1—37 sts.

Rnd 4: K17, work rnd 4 of chart over next 17 sts to marker, SM, knit to end.

Rnd 5: K17, work rnd 1 of chart over next 17 sts to marker, SM, M1, knit to end, M1—39 sts.

Rnd 6: K17, work rnd 2 of chart over next 17 sts to marker, SM, knit to end.

Rep rnds 3–6 twice more—47 sts; 34 sts for hand and 13 sts for thumb. Rep rnds 3 and 4 once more—49 sts; 34 sts for hand and 15 sts for thumb.

Make It Your Own!

You can easily add length to these mitts by repeating the chart to the desired length before starting the thumb gusset. Want more length on the hand? Add extra repeats of the chart after transferring stitches to the waste yarn for the thumb.

Hand

Next rnd: K17, work rnd 1 of chart over next 17 sts to marker, remove marker, place 15 sts on holder or waste yarn.

Work in established patt for another 3 rnds. Work ribbing rnd for 6 rnds. BO loosely in patt.

THUMB (BOTH MITTS)

Carefully transfer held sts from holder to dpns. Place 10 sts on needle 1, 5 sts on needle 2. With needle 3, pick up 3 sts in gap where thumb meets hand—18 sts total. Redistribute sts to 6 sts on each needle.

Rnds 1–3: Knit all sts.

Rnds 4–6: (K1, P1) to end.

BO thumb sts loosely in patt.

FINISHING

Block mitts to finished measurements given at beg of patt. With tapestry needle, weave in ends.

WRITTEN INSTRUCTIONS FOR CHART

If you prefer to follow row-by-row written instructions rather than a chart, use the following instructions.

Rnds 1 and 2: K1, P1, K13, P1, K1.

Rnd 3: K1, P1, K4tog, (YO, K1) 5 times, YO, ssssk, P1, K1.

Rnd 4: Rep rnd 1.

Rep rnds 1–4 for patt.

Astilbe chart

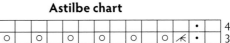

Legend

- ☐ K
- ☒ K4tog
- • P
- ☒ Ssssk
- ○ YO

LAPLACE

Designed and knit by author

This top-down crescent shawl features garter stitch worked between lace stitches.
Worsted-weight yarn makes this a very quick project!

SKILL LEVEL: Intermediate

FINISHED MEASUREMENTS:
74" x 19"

MATERIALS

3 skeins of Cadence from Hazel
Knits (100% superwash
merino wool; 110 g; 200
yards) in color Low Tide
4
US size 8 (5.0 mm) circular
needle, 32" cable or longer,
or size required for gauge
Tapestry needle
Blocking supplies

GAUGE

16 sts and 28 rows = 4" in
garter st

Gauge is not critical in this patt,
but a different gauge will affect
yardage and size of shawl.

PATTERN NOTES

Charts are on page 45. If you
prefer to follow written
instructions for the charted
material, see "Written
Instructions for Charts" on
page 44.

INSTRUCTIONS

Work garter-tab CO (page 90)
as follows:

CO 3 sts. Knit 10 rows. Turn
work 90° and pick up 5 sts
along edge. Turn work 90° and
pick up 3 sts from CO edge—11
sts total.

Row 1 (WS): K3, P5, K3.

Row 2 (RS): K3, (YO, K1) to last
3 sts, YO, K3—17 sts.

Row 3: K2, YO, K1, purl to the
last 3 sts, K1, YO, K2—19 sts.

Row 4: K3, YO, knit to the last 3
sts, YO, K3—21 sts.

Row 5: Rep row 3—23 sts.

Garter stitch and lace together again—my favorite!

Body of Shawl

Work rows 1–8 of chart A 10 times total—183 sts. Work rows 1–8 of chart B once—199 sts.

STITCH COUNT FOR BODY OF SHAWL	
Rep 1 of chart A	39 sts
Rep 2 of chart A	55 sts
Rep 3 of chart A	71 sts
Rep 4 of chart A	87 sts
Rep 5 of chart A	103 sts
Rep 6 of chart A	119 sts
Rep 7 of chart A	135 sts
Rep 8 of chart A	151 sts
Rep 9 of chart A	167 sts
Rep 10 of chart A	183 sts
Chart B	199 sts

Garter-Stitch Border

Row 1 (RS): K3, YO, knit to the last 3 sts, YO, K3—201 sts.

Row 2 (WS): K2, YO, knit to the last 2 sts, YO, K2—203 sts.

Rep rows 1 and 2 of garter-stitch border section another 11 times—247 sts.

FINISHING

BO loosely kw (page 91). Block shawl to finished measurements given at beg of patt. With tapestry needle, weave in ends.

WRITTEN INSTRUCTIONS FOR CHARTS

If you prefer to follow row-by-row written instructions rather than a chart, use the following instructions.

Chart A

Row 1 (RS): K3, YO, *K3, ssk, K3, YO, K1, YO, K3, K2tog, K2; rep from * to last 4 sts, K1, YO, K3.

Row 2 (WS): K2, YO, K3, *K2, P11, K3; rep from * to last 4 sts, K2, YO, K2.

Row 3: K3, YO, K2, *K3, ssk, K2, YO, K3, YO, K2, K2tog, K2; rep from * to last 6 sts, K3, YO, K3.

Row 4: K2, YO, K1, P1, K3, *K2, P11, K3; rep from * to last 6 sts, K2, P1, K1, YO, K2.

Row 5: K3, YO, K4, *K3, ssk, K1, YO, K5, YO, K1, K2tog, K2; rep from * to last 8 sts, K5, YO, K3.

Row 6: K2, YO, K1, P3, K3, *K2, P11, K3; rep from * to last 8 sts, K2, P3, K1, YO, K2.

Row 7: K3, YO, K6, *K3, ssk, YO, K7, YO, K2tog, K2; rep from * to last 10 sts, K7, YO, K3.

Row 8: K2, YO, K1, P5, K3, *K2, P11, K3; rep from * to last 10 sts, K2, P5, K1, YO, K2.

Rep rows 1–8 for patt.

Chart B

Row 1 (RS): K3, YO, *K3, ssk, K3, YO, K1, YO, K3, K2tog, K2; rep from * to last 4 sts, K1, YO, K3.

Row 2 (WS): K2, YO, K3, *K2, P5, K1, P5, K3; rep from * to last 4 sts, K2, YO, K2.

Row 3: K3, YO, K2, *K3, ssk, K2, YO, K3, YO, K2, K2tog, K2; rep from * to last 6 sts, K3, YO, K3.

Row 4: K2, YO, K1, P1, K3, *K2, P4, K3, P4, K3; rep from * to last 6 sts, K2, P1, K1, YO, K2.

Row 5: K3, YO, K4, *K3, ssk, K1, YO, K5, YO, K1, K2tog, K2; rep from * to last 8 sts, K5, YO, K3.

Row 6: K2, YO, K1, P3, K3, *K2, P3, K5, P3, K3; rep from * to last 8 sts, K2, P3, K1, YO, K2.

Row 7: K3, YO, K6, *K3, ssk, YO, K7, YO, K2tog, K2; rep from * to last 10 sts, K7, YO, K3.

Row 8: K2, YO, K1, P5, K3, *K2, P2, K7, P2, K3; rep from * to last 10 sts, K2, P5, K1, YO, K2.

Make It Your Own!

This shawl is easy to adjust to the size you want, making it a great project for substituting yarn weights. Work chart A to the desired length, and then work rows 1–8 of chart B once. You can also work the garter-stitch border to your desired length by repeating rows 1 and 2. Note that changing the size of the shawl and the yarn weight will affect the amount of yarn needed.

Laplace chart A

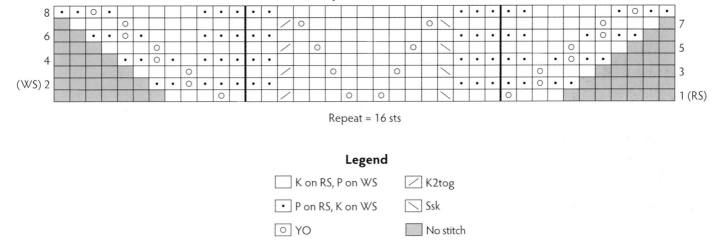

Repeat = 16 sts

Legend

☐	K on RS, P on WS	╱	K2tog
⊡	P on RS, K on WS	╲	Ssk
⊙	YO	▨	No stitch

Laplace chart B

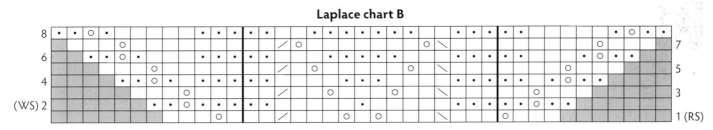

Repeat = 16 sts

Legend

☐	K on RS, P on WS	╱	K2tog
⊡	P on RS, K on WS	╲	Ssk
⊙	YO	▨	No stitch

GARNETT

Designed by author and knit by Melissa Rusk

A thick Aran-weight yarn is paired with triangle shaping in garter stitch for this shawl. This is the perfect piece when you want to be warm and cozy.

SKILL LEVEL: Intermediate

FINISHED MEASUREMENTS: 70" x 18"

MATERIALS

2 skeins of Cole from Anzula Luxury Fibers (70% silk, 30% camel; 100 g; 180 yards) in color Seabreeze **(4)**

US size 8 (5.0 mm) circular needle, 32" cable or longer

4 stitch markers

Tapestry needle

Blocking supplies

GAUGE

14 sts and 28 rows = 4" in garter st

Gauge is not critical in this patt, but a different gauge will affect yardage and size of shawl.

PATTERN NOTES

Charts are on page 49. If you prefer to follow written instructions for the charted material, see "Written Instructions for Charts" on page 48.

This project is worked primarily in garter stitch. You may find it helpful to use a stitch marker to indicate the right side of the work.

INSTRUCTIONS

Work garter-tab CO (page 90) as follows:

CO 3 sts. Knit 6 rows. Turn work 90° and pick up 3 sts along edge. Turn work 90° and pick up 3 sts from CO edge— 9 sts total.

Row 1 (WS): K3, PM, K1, PM, K1 (this is the center st), PM, K1, PM, K3.

Row 2 (RS): K3, SM, YO, knit to marker, YO, SM, K1, SM, YO, knit to last marker, YO, K3—13 sts.

Row 3: Knit all sts.

Rep rows 2 and 3 another 31 times (32 times total)—137 sts. Rep row 2 once more—141 sts.

Next row (WS): K3, remove marker, knit to next marker, remove marker, K1f&b, remove marker, knit to final marker, remove marker, K3—142 sts.

Work charts as follows:

Chart A—158 sts

Chart B—174 sts

Chart A—190 sts

Chart B—206 sts

Chart A—222 sts

Chart B—238 sts

Work final garter-st band as follows:

(Worked same on both RS and WS)

Rows 1–8: K3, YO, knit to the last 3 sts, YO, K3—254 sts.

FINISHING

BO loosely kw (page 91). Block shawl to finished measurements given at beg of patt. With tapestry needle, weave in ends.

WRITTEN INSTRUCTIONS FOR CHARTS

If you prefer to follow row-by-row written instructions rather than a chart, use the following instructions.

Chart A

Row 1 (RS): K3, YO, *K8, (K2tog, YO) 4 times; rep from * to last 11 sts, K8, YO, K3.

Row 2 (WS): K3, YO, K9, *P8, K8; rep from * to last 4 sts, K1, YO, K3.

Row 3: K3, YO, K2, *K8, (K2tog, YO) 4 times; rep from * to last 13 sts, K10, YO, K3.

Row 4: K3, YO, K1, P2, K8, *P8, K8; rep from * to last 6 sts, P2, K1, YO, K3.

Row 5: K3, YO, K2, K2tog, YO, *K8, (K2tog, YO) 4 times; rep from * to last 15 sts, K8, K2tog, YO, K2, YO, K3.

Row 6: K3, YO, K1, P4, K8, *P8, K8; rep from * to last 8 sts, P4, K1, YO, K3.

Row 7: K3, YO, K2, (K2tog, YO) twice, *K8, (K2tog, YO) 4 times; rep from * to last 17 sts, K8, (K2tog, YO) twice, K2, YO, K3.

Row 8: K3, YO, K1, P6, K8, *P8, K8; rep from * to last 10 sts, P6, K1, YO, K3.

Chart B

Row 1 (RS): K3, YO, *K8, (YO, ssk) 4 times; rep from * to last 11 sts, K8, YO, K3.

Row 2 (WS): K3, YO, K9, *P8, K8; rep from * to last 4 sts, K1, YO, K3.

Row 3: K3, YO, K2, *K8, (YO, ssk) 4 times; rep from * to last 13 sts, K10, YO, K3.

Row 4: K3, YO, K1, P2, K8, *P8, K8; rep from * to last 6 sts, P2, K1, YO, K3.

Row 5: K3, YO, K2, YO, ssk, *K8, (YO, ssk) 4 times; rep from * to last 15 sts, K8, YO, ssk, K2, YO, K3.

Row 6: K3, YO, K1, P4, K8, *P8, K8; rep from * to last 8 sts, P4, K1, YO, K3.

Row 7: K3, YO, K2, (YO, ssk) twice, *K8, (YO, ssk) 4 times; rep from * to last 17 sts, K8, (YO, ssk) twice, K2, YO, K3.

Row 8: K3, YO, K1, P6, K8, *P8, K8; rep from * to last 10 sts, P6, K1, YO, K3.

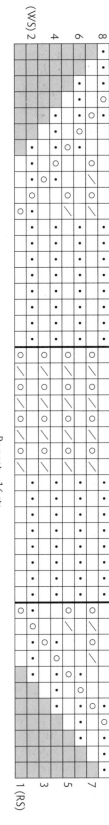

Garnett chart A

Repeat = 16 sts

Legend

	K on RS, P on WS		K2tog
•	P on RS, K on WS		No stitch
○	YO		

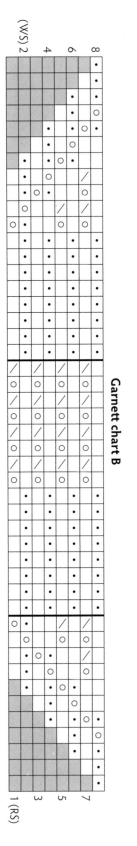

Garnett chart B

Repeat = 16 sts

Legend

	K on RS, P on WS		Ssk
•	P on RS, K on WS		No stitch
○	YO		

MONTGOMERY

Designed and knit by author

A beautiful cable panel runs along the back of these mittens. Only two cable stitches are used, making this design look much more complicated than it is!

SKILL LEVEL: Intermediate

FINISHED CIRCUMFERENCE: 7", fits up to 8½"

FINISHED LENGTH: 13"

MATERIALS

1 skein of Wool-Ease from Lion Brand (80% acrylic, 20% wool; 85 g; 197 yards) in color Rose Heather (**4**)
Set of 5 double-pointed needles in US size 6 (4.0 mm) or size required for gauge
2 stitch markers
Stitch holder or waste yarn
Tapestry needle

GAUGE

20 sts and 28 rows = 4" in St st

PATTERN NOTES

Chart is on page 53. If you prefer to follow written instructions for the charted material, see "Written Instructions for Chart" on page 53.

Take note to use "left mitten" and "right mitten" instructions when necessary. If no left/right indication is given, work the same for both mitts.

SPECIAL ABBREVIATIONS

2/2 RC: Sl 2 sts to cable needle, hold in back, K2, K2 from cable needle

2/2 LC: Sl 2 sts to cable needle, hold in front, K2, K2 from cable needle

INSTRUCTIONS (MAKE 2.)

CO 40 sts. Divide stitches evenly on 4 dpns. Join in the round, being careful not to twist sts. PM to mark beg of rnd.

Ribbing rnd: *(K1, P1) twice, K2, P2, K4, P2, K2, (P1, K1) twice; rep from * once more to end of rnd.

Rep ribbing rnd for 23 more rnds (24 rnds total).

LEFT MITTEN

Set-up rnd: K3, P1, K12, P1, knit to end.

Work mitten as follows.

Rnd 1: Work rnd 1 of chart over next 20 sts, knit to end of rnd.

Rnd 2: Work rnd 2 of chart over next 20 sts, knit to end of rnd.

Cont working left mitten in established patt, working next subsequent rnd of chart until chart has been completed 1 time (16 rnds total).

Thumb Gusset

Rnd 1: Work rnd 1 of chart over next 20 sts, knit to end, PM, M1—41 sts.

Rnd 2: Work rnd 2 of chart over next 20 sts, knit to marker, SM, K1.

Rnd 3: Work next rnd of chart over next 20 sts, knit to marker, SM, M1, knit to end, M1—43 sts.

Rnd 4: Work next rnd of chart over next 20 sts, knit to marker, SM, knit to end.

Rep last 2 rnds, working next subsequent rnd of chart another 5 times—53 sts; 40 sts for hand and 13 sts for thumb.

Next rnd: Work next rnd (rnd 15) of chart over next 20 sts, knit to marker, remove marker, place 13 sts on holder or waste yarn.

Next rnd: Work next rnd (rnd 16) of chart over next 20 sts, knit to end of rnd.

Hand

Cont working in established patt for another 32 rnds.

Dec as follows.

Rnd 1: *K1, ssk, K14, K2tog, K1; rep from * once more to end of rnd—36 sts.

Rnd 2: *K1, ssk, K12, K2tog, K1; rep from * once more to end of rnd—32 sts.

Rnd 3: *K1, ssk, K10, K2tog, K1; rep from * once more to end of rnd—28 sts.

Rnd 4: *K1, ssk, K8, K2tog, K1; rep from * once more to end of rnd—24 sts.

Rnd 5: *K1, ssk, K6, K2tog, K1; rep from * once more to end of rnd—20 sts.

Rnd 6: *K1, ssk, K4, K2tog, K1; rep from * once more to end of rnd—16 sts.

Rearrange sts so that 8 sts for back of hand are on 1 dpn and 8 sts for palm are on another. Use Kitchener st to graft together. (You can visit ShopMartingale.com/HowtoKnit for Kitchener st instructions.)

RIGHT MITTEN

Set-up rnd: K23, P1, K12, P1, K3.

Work mitten as follows.

Rnd 1: K20, work rnd 1 of chart over next 20 sts to end of rnd.

Rnd 2: K20, work rnd 2 of chart over next 20 sts to end of rnd.

Cont working right mitten in established patt, working next subsequent rnd of chart until chart has been completed 1 time (16 rnds total).

Thumb Gusset

Rnd 1: K20, work rnd 1 of chart over next 20 sts to end, PM, M1—41 sts.

Rnd 2: K20, work rnd 2 of chart over next 20 sts to marker, SM, K1.

Rnd 3: K20, work next rnd of chart over next 20 sts to marker, SM, M1, knit to end, M1—43 sts.

Rnd 4: K20, work next rnd of chart over next 20 sts to marker, SM, knit to end.

Rep last 2 rnds, working next subsequent rnd of chart another 5 times—53 sts; 40 sts for hand and 13 sts for thumb.

Next rnd: K20, work next rnd (rnd 15) of chart over next 20 sts to marker, remove marker, place 13 sts on holder or waste yarn.

Next rnd: K20, work next rnd (rnd 16) of chart over next 20 sts to end of rnd.

Hand

Cont working in established patt for another 32 rnds.

Dec as follows.

Rnd 1: *K1, ssk, K14, K2tog, K1; rep from * once more to end of rnd—36 sts.

Rnd 2: *K1, ssk, K12, K2tog, K1; rep from * once more to end of rnd—32 sts.

Rnd 3: *K1, ssk, K10, K2tog, K1; rep from * once more to end of rnd—28 sts.

Rnd 4: *K1, ssk, K8, K2tog, K1; rep from * once more to end of rnd—24 sts.

Rnd 5: *K1, ssk, K6, K2tog, K1; rep from * once more to end of rnd—20 sts.

Rnd 6: *K1, ssk, K4, K2tog, K1; rep from * once more to end of rnd—16 sts.

Rearrange sts so that 8 sts for back of hand are on 1 dpn and 8 sts for palm are on another. Use Kitchener st to graft together.

THUMB (BOTH MITTENS)

Carefully transfer held sts from holder to dpns. Place 6 sts on needle 1, 7 sts on needle 2. With needle 3, pick up 5 sts in gap where thumb meets hand—18 sts total. Redistribute sts to 6 sts on each needle.

Rnds 1–12: Knit all sts.

Next rnd: (K2tog) to end of rnd—9 sts.

Next rnd: Knit all sts.

Next rnd: K1, (K2tog) to end of rnd—5 sts.

Cut yarn, leaving 6" tail. Thread yarn onto tapestry needle and thread through rem sts. Gather sts and tie off.

FINISHING

Block mittens to finished measurements given at beg of patt. With tapestry needle, weave in ends.

WRITTEN INSTRUCTIONS FOR CHART

If you prefer to follow row-by-row written instructions rather than a chart, use the following instructions.

Rnd 1: K3, P1, K2, 2/2 RC, 2/2 LC, K2, P1, K3.

Rnd 2 and all even-numbered rnds: K3, P1, K12, P1, K3.

Rnd 3: K3, P1, 2/2 RC, K4, 2/2 LC, P1, K3.

Rnd 5: Rep rnd 1.

Rnd 7: Rep rnd 3.

Rnd 9: K3, P1, 2/2 LC, K4, 2/2 RC, P1, K3.

Rnd 11: K3, P1, K2, 2/2 LC, 2/2 RC, K2, P1, K3.

Rnd 13: Rep rnd 9.

Rnd 15: Rep rnd 11.

Rnd 16: K3, P1, K12, P1, K3.

Rep rnds 1–16 for patt.

Montgomery chart

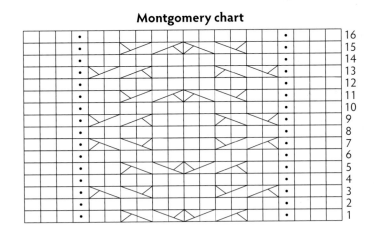

Legend

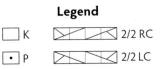

☐ K   2/2 RC

☐• P   2/2 LC

TIMBERLINE

Designed by author and knit by Cathy Rusk

Worked from the bottom up, this short-row shawl is quick to knit and fun to wear.
A vertical lace pattern with paired decreases adds texture to the bottom of the piece.

SKILL LEVEL: Intermediate

FINISHED MEASUREMENTS:
15" x 52"

MATERIALS

3 skeins of For Better or
   Worsted from Anzula
   Luxury Fibers (80%
   superwash merino, 10%
   cashmere, 10% nylon; 115 g;
   200 yards) in color Bark
   【4】
US size 8 (5.0 mm) circular
   needle, 32" cable or longer
Tapestry needle
Blocking supplies

GAUGE

14 sts and 28 rows = 4" in St st

Gauge is not critical in this patt,
but a different gauge will affect
yardage and size of shawl.

PATTERN NOTES

Charts are on page 57. If you
prefer to follow written
instructions for the charted
material, see "Written
Instructions for Charts" on
page 57.

INSTRUCTIONS

CO 253 sts. Work chart A twice
(32 rows). Work chart B once
(16 rows)—181 sts.

Row 1 (RS): K95, turn work (86
sts unworked).

Row 2 (WS): P9, turn work (86
sts unworked).

Row 3: K8, ssk, K3, turn work
(82 sts unworked)—180 sts
total.

The vertical lace pattern reminds me of walking along a nearby park trail and coming to the edge of the woods lined with big, beautiful trees.

Row 4: P11, P2tog, P3, turn work (82 sts unworked)—179 sts total.

Row 5: Knit to 1 st before gap (1 st before previous turning point), ssk, K3, turn work.

Row 6: Purl to 1 st before gap (1 st before previous turning point), P2tog, P3, turn work.

Rep rows 5 and 6 another 19 times (2 sts rem unworked on each end—139 sts rem).

Next row (RS): Knit to 1 st before gap (1 st before previous turning point), ssk, K1—138 sts.

Rep last row on WS—137 sts.

Knit 6 rows.

Make It Your Own!

Chart A can be repeated as many times as you like before moving on to chart B. This shawl would also look stunning in a bulky-weight yarn! Just remember that adding chart repeats or changing yarns will affect the amount of yarn needed.

FINISHING

BO loosely kw (page 91). Block shawl to finished measurements given at beg of patt. With tapestry needle, weave in ends.

WRITTEN INSTRUCTIONS FOR CHARTS

If you prefer to follow row-by-row written instructions rather than a chart, use the following instructions.

Chart A

Rows 1, 3, 5, 7, 9, 11, and 13 (RS): K2, YO, ssk, *K2tog, YO, K3, YO, ssk; rep from * to last 4 sts, K2tog, YO, K2.

Rows 2, 4, 6, 8, 10, and 12 (WS): K2, purl to the last 2 sts, K2.

Rows 14–16: Knit all sts.

Rep rows 1–16 for patt.

Chart B

Rows 1, 3, 5, 7, 9, and 11 (RS): K2, YO, ssk, *K2tog, YO, K3, YO, ssk; rep from * to last 4 sts, K2tog, YO, K2.

Rows 2, 4, 6, 8, 10, and 12 (WS): K2, purl to the last 2 sts, K2.

Row 13: K2, ssk, *K2tog, K3, ssk; rep from * to last 4 sts, K2tog, K2.

Rows 14–16: Knit all sts.

Timberline chart A

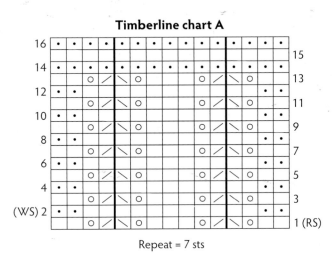

Repeat = 7 sts

Legend

☐ K on RS, P on WS

· P on RS, K on WS

○ YO

╱ K2tog

╲ Ssk

Timberline chart B

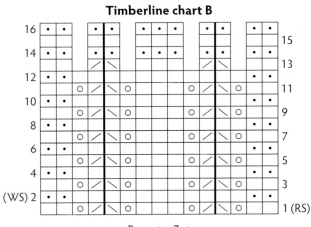

Repeat = 7 sts

Legend

☐ K on RS, P on WS

· P on RS, K on WS

○ YO

╱ K2tog

╲ Ssk

CRAWFORD

Designed by author and knit by Jenni Lesniak

This pretty and versatile scarf will become your essential accessory for chilly days. The design is knit on the bias, creating distinctive diagonal cables running through it.

SKILL LEVEL: Experienced

FINISHED MEASUREMENTS: 8" x 72"

MATERIALS

2 skeins of Erin from Imperial Yarn (100% wool; 113 g; 225 yards) in color 326 Denim Dusk **4**

US size 8 (5.0 mm) knitting needles, or size required for gauge

Cable needle

Tapestry needle

Blocking supplies

GAUGE

14 sts and 26 rows = 4" in rev St st

Gauge is not critical in this patt, but a different gauge will affect yardage and size of scarf.

SPECIAL ABBREVIATION

2/2 RC: Slip 2 sts to cable needle, hold in back, K2, K2 from cable needle

PATTERN NOTES

Charts are on pages 62 and 63. If you prefer to follow written instructions for the charted material, see "Written Instructions for Charts" on page 60.

INSTRUCTIONS

CO 6 sts. Knit 1 row on WS.

Work chart A—36 sts.

Work chart B until piece measures 66" from CO, ending with row 18.

Note: Stitch count remains 36 sts for all of chart B.

Work chart C—6 sts. Knit 1 row on RS.

FINISHING

BO loosely kw (page 91). Block scarf to finished measurements given at beg of patt. With tapestry needle, weave in ends.

WRITTEN INSTRUCTIONS FOR CHARTS

If you prefer to follow row-by-row written instructions rather than a chart, use the following instructions.

Chart A

Row 1 (RS): (K2, M1) twice, K2—8 sts.

Row 2 (WS): K2, P4, K2.

Row 3: K2, M1, K4, M1, K2—10 sts.

Row 4: K2, P6, K2.

Row 5: K2, M1, K1, 2/2 RC, K1, M1, K2—12 sts.

Row 6: K2, P1, K1, P4, K1, P1, K2.

Row 7: K2, M1, K1, P1, K4, P1, K1, M1, K2—14 sts.

Row 8: K2, P1, K2, P4, K2, P1, K2.

Row 9: K2, M1, K1, P2, K4, P2, K1, M1, K2—16 sts.

Row 10: K2, P1, K3, P4, K3, P1, K2.

Row 11: K2, M1, K1, P3, 2/2 RC, P3, K1, M1, K2—18 sts.

Row 12: K2, P1, K4, P4, K4, P1, K2.

Row 13: K2, M1, K1, P4, K4, P4, K1, M1, K2—20 sts.

Row 14: K2, P1, K5, P4, K5, P1, K2.

Row 15: K2, M1, K1, P5, K4, P5, K1, M1, K2—22 sts.

Row 16: K2, P2, K5, P4, K5, P2, K2.

Row 17: K2, M1, K2, P5, 2/2 RC, P5, K2, M1, K2—24 sts.

Row 18: K2, P3, K5, P4, K5, P3, K2.

Row 19: K2, M1, K3, P5, K4, P5, K3, M1, K2—26 sts.

Row 20: K2, (P4, K5) twice, P4, K2.

Row 21: K2, M1, (K4, P5) twice, K4, M1, K2—28 sts.

Row 22: K2, P5, K5, P4, K5, P5, K2.

Row 23: K2, M1, K1, (2/2 RC, P5) twice, 2/2 RC, K1, M1, K2—30 sts.

Row 24: K2, P1, K1, (P4, K5) twice, P4, K1, P1, K2.

Row 25: K2, M1, K1, P1, (K4, P5) twice, K4, P1, K1, M1, K2—32 sts.

Row 26: K2, P1, K2, (P4, K5) twice, P4, K2, P1, K2.

Row 27: K2, M1, K1, P2, (K4, P5) twice, K4, P2, K1, M1, K2—34 sts.

Row 28: K2, P1, K3, (P4, K5) twice, P4, K3, P1, K2.

Row 29: K2, M1, K1, P3, (2/2 RC, P5) twice, 2/2 RC, P3, K1, M1, K2—36 sts.

Row 30: K2, P1, K4, (P4, K5) twice, P4, K4, P1, K2.

Chart B

Note: St count is 36 for entire chart.

Row 1 (RS): K2, M1, K1, P4, (K4, P5) twice, K4, P3, ssk, K2.

Row 2 (WS): K2, P1, K3, (P4, K5) 3 times, P1, K2.

Row 3: K2, M1, K1, (P5, K4) 3 times, P2, ssk, K2.

Row 4: K2, P1, K2, (P4, K5) 3 times, P2, K2.

Row 5: K2, M1, K2, (P5, 2/2 RC) 3 times, P1, ssk, K2.

Row 6: K2, P1, K1, (P4, K5) 3 times, P3, K2.

Row 7: K2, M1, K3, (P5, K4) 3 times, ssk, K2.

Row 8: K2, P5, (K5, P4) 3 times, K2.

Row 9: K2, M1, (K4, P5) twice, K5, P4, K3, ssk, K2.

Row 10: K2, (P4, K5) 3 times, P5, K2.

Row 11: K2, M1, K1, (2/2 RC, P5) 3 times, K2, ssk, K2.

Row 12: K2, P3, (K5, P4) 3 times, K1, P1, K2.

Row 13: K2, M1, K1, P1, (K4, P5) 3 times, K1, ssk, K2.

Row 14: K2, P2, (K5, P4) 3 times, K2, P1, K2.

Row 15: K2, M1, K1, P2, (K4, P5) twice, K4, P4, K1, ssk, K2.

Row 16: K2, P2, K4, (P4, K5) twice, P4, K3, P1, K2.

Row 17: K2, M1, K1, P3, (2/2 RC, P5) twice, 2/2 RC, P3, K1, ssk, K2.

Row 18: K2, P2, K3, (P4, K5) twice, P4, K4, P1, K2.

Rep rows 1–18 for patt.

Chart C

Row 1 (RS): K2, K2tog, P3, (K4, P5) twice, K4, P3, ssk, K2. (34 sts)

Row 2 (WS): K2, P1, K3, (P4, K5) twice, P4, K3, P1, K2.

Row 3: K2, K2tog, P2, (K4, P5) twice, K4, P2, ssk, K2. (32 sts)

Row 4: K2, P1, K2, (P4, K5) twice, P4, K2, P1, K2.

Row 5: K2, K2tog, P1, (2/2 RC, P5) twice, 2/2 RC, P1, ssk, K2. (30 sts)

Row 6: K2, P1, K1, (P4, K5) twice, P4, K1, P1, K2.

Row 7: K2, K2tog, (K4, P5) twice, K4, ssk, K2—28 sts.

Row 8: K2, P5, K5, P4, K5, P5, K2.

Row 9: K2, K2tog, K3, P5, K4, P5, K3, ssk, K2—26 sts.

Row 10: K2, (P4, K5) twice, P4, K2.

Row 11: K2, K2tog, K2, P5, 2/2 RC, P5, K2, ssk, K2—24 sts.

Row 12: K2, P3, K5, P4, K5, P3, K2.

Row 13: K2, K2tog, K1, P5, K4, P5, K1, ssk, K2—22 sts.

Row 14: K2, P2, K5, P4, K5, P2, K2.

Row 15: K2, K2tog, P5, K4, P5, ssk, K2—20 sts.

Row 16: K2, P1, K5, P4, K5, P1, K2.

Row 17: K2, K2tog, P4, 2/2 RC, P4, ssk, K2—18 sts.

Row 18: K2, P1, K4, P4, K4, P1, K2.

Row 19: K2, K2tog, P3, K4, P3, ssk, K2—16 sts.

Row 20: K2, P1, K3, P4, K3, P1, K2.

Row 21: K2, K2tog, P2, K4, P2, ssk, K2—14 sts.

Row 22: K2, P1, K2, P4, K2, P1, K2.

Row 23: K2, K2tog, P1, 2/2 RC, P1, ssk, K2—12 sts.

Row 24: K2, P1, K1, P4, K1, P1, K2.

Row 25: K2, K2tog, K4, ssk, K2—10 sts.

Row 26: K2, P6, K2.

Row 27: K2, K2tog, K2, ssk, K2—8 sts.

Row 28: K2, P4, K2.

Row 29: K2, K2tog, ssk, K2—6 sts.

Row 30: K2, P2, K2.

Crawford chart A

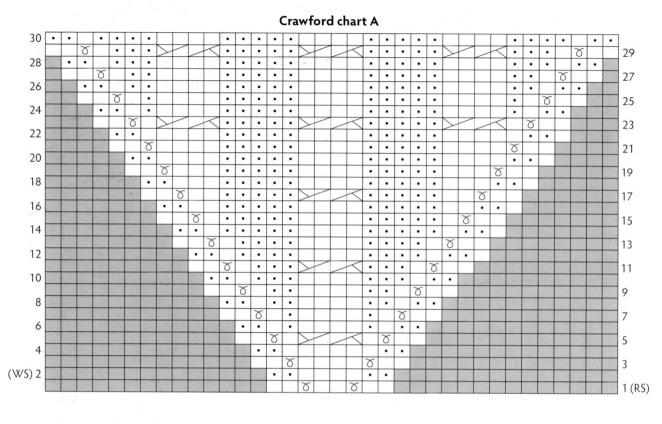

Legend

☐ K on RS, P on WS	◨◩ 2/2 RC
⊡ P on RS, K on WS	▨ No stitch
୪ M1	

Crawford chart B

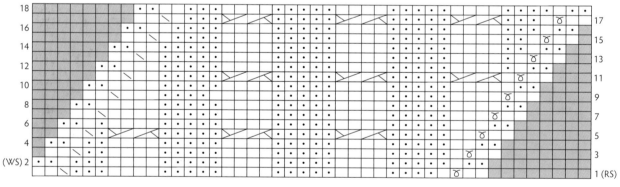

Legend

☐ K on RS, P on WS	◨◩ 2/2 RC
⊡ P on RS, K on WS	◹ Ssk
୪ M1	▨ No stitch

Cozy Stash-Busting Knits

Crawford chart C

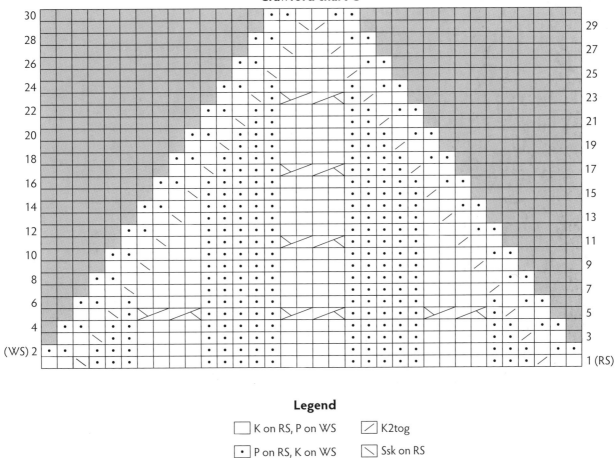

Legend

☐	K on RS, P on WS
⊡	P on RS, K on WS
⧄	2/2 RC
╱	K2tog
╲	Ssk on RS
▨	No stitch

ASTRID

Designed and knit by author

*Slipped-stitch cables are my new obsession, and this sweet hat is the perfect showcase
for them. I love the texture and interest they create in an otherwise simple cable.
I also love that the slipped stitches make it very easy to cable without a cable needle.*

SKILL LEVEL: Intermediate

SIZES: Adult Small (Adult Large)

FINISHED CIRCUMFERENCE: 19",
fits up to 21" (22", fits up to 24")

FINISHED LENGTH: 8½ (10)"

MATERIALS

1 (2) skein(s) of Canopy
Worsted from The Fibre
Company (50% baby
alpaca, 30% merino, 20%
viscose bamboo; 100 g; 200
yards) in color Guava (4)

US size 6 (4.0 mm) circular
needle, 16" cable, or size
required for gauge
Set of 5 double-pointed needles
in US size 6 (4.0 mm) or
size required for gauge
1 stitch marker
Tapestry needle

GAUGE

20 sts and 28 rows = 4" in
chart patt, slightly stretched

SPECIAL ABBREVIATIONS

1/2 LC: Sl 1 st to cable needle,
hold in front, K2, K1 from cable
needle

1/2 RC: Sl 2 sts to cable needle,
hold in back, K1, K2 from cable
needle

PATTERN NOTES

Chart is on page 66. If you
prefer to follow written
instructions for the charted
material, see "Written
Instructions for Chart" on
page 66.

The pattern is written for the
Adult Small with the
instructions for Adult Large
written in parentheses ( ),
where necessary. If only one

instruction is given, it should be worked for both sizes. Adult Small is shown.

INSTRUCTIONS

With circular needle, CO 108 (126) sts. Join in the round, being careful not to twist sts. PM to mark start of rnd.

Ribbing rnd: *K3, P1, K3, P2; rep from * to end of rnd.

Work ribbing rnd for another 9 (13) rnds.

Work rnds 1–6 of chart 7 (8) times—42 (48) rnds total. Dec as follows.

Note: Switch to dpns when stitches no longer comfortably fit on 16" circular needles.

Rnd 1: *Ssk, K1, P1, K1, K2tog, P2; rep from * to end of rnd— 84 (98) sts.

Rnd 2: *K2, P1, K2, P2; rep from * to end of rnd.

Rnd 3: *Ssk, P1, K2tog, P2; rep from * to end of rnd—60 (70) sts.

Rnd 4: *K3, P2; rep from * to end of rnd.

Rnd 5: *Sk2p, P2; rep from * to end of rnd—36 (42) sts.

Rnd 6: *K1, K2tog; rep from * to end of rnd—24 (28) sts.

Rnd 7: *K2tog; rep from * to end of rnd—12 (14) sts.

FINISHING

Cut yarn, leaving 8" tail. Thread yarn onto tapestry needle and thread through rem sts. Gather sts and tie off. Weave in ends.

WRITTEN INSTRUCTIONS FOR CHART

Rnds 1 and 2: *Sl 1 wyib, K2, P1, K2, sl 1 wyib, P2; rep from * to end of rnd.

Rnd 3: 1/2 LC, P1, 1/2 RC, P2; rep from * to end of rnd.

Rnds 4–6: K3, P1, K3, P2; rep from * to end of rnd.

Rep rnds 1–6 for patt.

Astrid chart

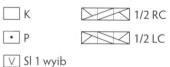

Repeat = 9 sts

Legend

☐ K		⧄ 1/2 RC
• P		⧄ 1/2 LC
V Sl 1 wyib		

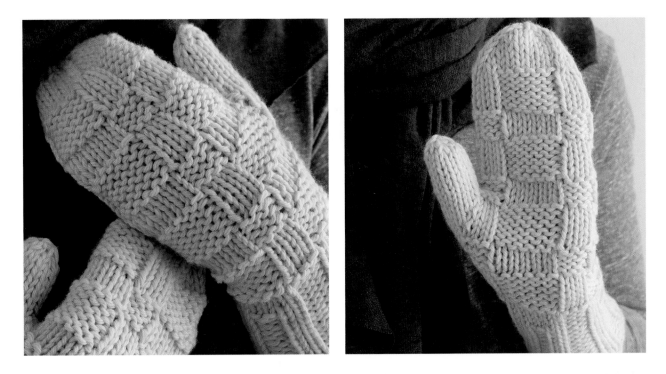

FLANNER

Designed and knit by author

As I knit these bulky mittens, all I could think about was how I could have used a pair like this when I was in college many years ago. Those long walks to the chemistry building along the Chicago lakefront sure were chilly!

SKILL LEVEL: Intermediate

FINISHED CIRCUMFERENCE: 6½", fits up to 8½"

FINISHED LENGTH: 12"

MATERIALS

1 skein of Vintage Chunky from Berroco (52% acrylic, 40% wool, 8% nylon; 100 g; 136 yards) in color 6113 Misty 【5】

Set of 4 double-pointed needles US size 9 (5.5 mm), or size required for gauge

2 stitch markers
Stitch holder or waste yarn
Tapestry needle

GAUGE

16 sts and 20 rows = 4" in chart patt in the round

PATTERN NOTES

Charts are on page 69. If you prefer to follow written instructions for the charted material, see "Written Instructions for Charts" on page 69.

The mittens are mirror images of each other, so be sure to use the correct chart when knitting each mitten.

RIGHT MITTEN

CO 27 sts. Divide stitches evenly on 3 dpns. Join in the round, being careful not to twist sts. PM to mark beg of rnd.

Ribbing rnd: *K2, P2, K2, P3; rep from * to end of rnd.

Rep ribbing rnd for 14 more rnds (15 rnds total).

Working right mitten chart patt 3 times on each rnd, work chart 1 time—24 rnds total.

Thumb Gusset

Rnd 1: Work rnd 1 of right mitten chart to end of rnd, PM, M1—28 sts.

Rnd 2: Work rnd 2 of right mitten chart to marker, SM, K1.

Rnd 3: Work next rnd of right mitten chart to marker, SM, M1, knit to end, M1—30 sts.

Rnd 4: Work next rnd of right mitten chart to marker, SM, knit to end.

Cont working in patt for right mitten chart on subsequent rows (starting with rnd 5), rep last 2 rnds another 3 times—36 sts (27 sts for hand and 9 sts for thumb).

Hand

Next rnd: Work next rnd (1) of right mitten chart to marker, remove marker, place 9 sts on stitch holder or waste yarn.

Work in established right mitten chart patt for another 19 rnds.

Dec for top of mitten as follows.

Rnd 1: *K7, K2tog; rep from * to end of rnd—24 sts.

Rnd 2: Knit all sts.

Rnd 3: *K6, K2tog; rep from * to end of rnd—21 sts.

Rnd 4: Knit all sts.

Rnd 5: *K5, K2tog; rep from * to end of rnd—18 sts.

Rnd 6: *K4, K2tog; rep from * to end of rnd—15 sts.

Rnd 7: K1, *K2tog, rep from * to end of rnd—8 sts.

Cut yarn, leaving 8" tail. Thread yarn onto tapestry needle and thread through rem sts. Gather sts and tie off.

Thumb

Carefully transfer held sts from holder to dpns. Place 5 sts on needle 1, 4 sts on needle 2. With needle 3, pick up 3 sts in gap where thumb meets hand—12 sts total. Redistribute sts to 4 sts on each needle.

Rnds 1-6: Knit all sts.

Rnd 7: [K2tog] around—6 sts.

Rnd 8: [K2tog] around—3 sts.

Cut yarn, leaving 8" tail. Thread yarn onto tapestry needle and thread through rem sts. Gather sts and tie off.

LEFT MITTEN

Using left mitten chart, work left mitten same as right mitten.

FINISHING

Block mitts to finished measurements given at beg of patt. With tapestry needle, weave in ends.

WRITTEN INSTRUCTIONS FOR CHARTS

If you prefer to follow row-by-row written instructions rather than a chart, use the following instructions.

Right Mitten

Rnds 1–4: *P3, K6; rep from * to end of rnd.

Rnds 5–10: *K3, P6; rep from * to end of rnd.

Rep rnds 1–10 for patt.

Left Mitten

Rnds 1–4: *K6, P3; rep from * to end of rnd.

Rnds 5–10: *P6, K3; rep from * to end of rnd.

Rep rnds 1–10 for patt.

Flanner right mitten chart

Repeat = 9 sts

Flanner left mitten chart

Repeat = 9 sts

Legend

☐ K

⊡ P

FILIGREE

Designed and knit by author

Living in the Midwest, I find that a chunky ear warmer is a must-have, and this lace ear warmer is the perfect addition to my wardrobe. The lace pattern features an interesting decrease, making the holes small to cut down on drafts. To add extra warmth, sew coordinating fleece to the wrong side of the piece.

SKILL LEVEL: Easy

FINISHED MEASUREMENTS:
5½" x 18" (stretches up to 21")

MATERIALS

1 skein of Outer from Spud & Chloe (65% superwash wool, 35% organic cotton; 100 g; 60 yards), in color 7211 Rocket (**6**)
US size 11 (8.0 mm) knitting needles, or size required for gauge
Tapestry needle
2 buttons, 1" diameter

GAUGE

11 sts and 15 rows = 4" in patt

PATTERN NOTES

Ear warmer is written for one size and will stretch to fit a variety of heads. To make a smaller ear warmer, work pattern as written until piece is 2" shorter than desired length, ending with a WS row. Work final button band (starting with row 11) to finish.

INSTRUCTIONS

CO 9 sts. Knit 1 row on WS.

Row 1 (RS): K2, M1L, knit to the last 2 sts, M1R, K2—11 sts.

Row 2 (WS): Knit all sts.

Rep rows 1 and 2 twice more—15 sts.

Row 7: K2, *YO, K3, with LH needle lift first st of the 3 sts just knit over the last 2 sts; rep from * to last st, K1.

Two buttons hold the ear warmer securely in place.

Row 8: K1, P13, K1.

Row 9: K1, *K3, with LH needle lift first st of the 3 sts just knit over the last 2 sts, YO; rep from * to last 2 sts, K2.

Row 10: Rep row 8.

Rep rows 7–10 until piece measures 16" from CO, ending with row 8 or 10.

Row 11: K2, ssk, knit to last 4 sts, K2tog, K2—13 sts.

Row 12: Knit all sts.

Row 13: K2, ssk, YO, K2tog, K1, ssk, YO, K2tog, K2—11 sts.

Row 14: Knit all sts.

Row 15: Rep row 11—9 sts.

Row 16: Knit all sts.

FINISHING

BO loosely kw (page 91) on WS. If desired, block piece. With tapestry needle, weave in ends. Sew buttons on button band to match up with corresponding buttonhole.

WANDERER

Designed and knit by author

If you look up cozy in the dictionary, there very well might be a photo of Wanderer. Knit in a lovely, bulky yarn and with cables running between the lace motifs, this shawl defines comfy.

SKILL LEVEL: Intermediate

FINISHED MEASUREMENTS:
56" x 28"

MATERIALS

3 skeins of Wool of the Andes Superwash Bulky from Knit Picks (100% superwash wool; 100 g; 137 yards) in color Persimmon Heather 🔵**5**

US size 9 (5.5 mm) circular needle, 32" cable or longer, or size required for gauge
4 stitch markers

Cable needle
Tapestry needle
Blocking supplies

GAUGE

12 sts and 20 rows = 4" in St st

Gauge is not critical in this patt, but a different gauge will affect yardage and size of shawl.

SPECIAL ABBREVIATION

3/3 LC: Slip 3 sts to cable needle, hold in front, K3, K3 from cable needle

PATTERN NOTES

Charts are on page 75. If you prefer to follow written instructions for the charted material, see "Written Instructions for Charts" on page 74.

INSTRUCTIONS

Work garter-tab CO (page 90) as follows:

CO 3 sts. Knit 10 rows. Turn work 90° and pick up 5 sts along edge. Turn work 90° and pick up 3 sts from CO edge—11 sts total.

Body of Shawl

Row 1 (WS): K3, P5, K3.

Row 2 (RS): K3, PM, YO, K2, YO, PM, K1 (this is the center st), PM, YO, K2; YO, PM, K3—15 sts.

Row 3: K3, purl to the last 3 sts, K3.

Row 4: K3, SM, YO, knit to next marker, YO, SM, K1, SM, YO, knit to last 3 sts, YO, SM, K3—19 sts.

Rep rows 3 and 4 another 24 times—115 sts. Rep row 3 once more.

Lace Edging

Cont working first 3 sts and last 3 sts in garter st (knit every row). Work the center st in St st (knit on RS, purl on WS). Work charts in between stitch markers on each half of shawl as follows.

Chart A—131 sts

Chart B—159 sts

Chart B—187 sts

Chart C—199 sts

FINISHING

BO loosely kw (page 91) on RS. Block shawl to finished measurements given at beg of patt. With tapestry needle, weave in ends.

WRITTEN INSTRUCTIONS FOR CHARTS

If you prefer to follow row-by-row written instructions rather than a chart, use the following instructions.

Chart A

Row 1 (RS): YO, K3, *K2, YO, K2tog, K10; rep from * to 9 sts before marker, K2, YO, K2tog, K5, YO.

Row 2 and all even-numbered rows (WS): Purl all sts.

Row 3: YO, K4, *K1, (YO, K2tog) twice, K9; rep from * to 10 sts before marker, K1, (YO, K2tog) twice, K5, YO.

Row 5: YO, K5, *(YO, K2tog) 3 times, K8; rep from * to 11 sts before marker, (YO, K2tog) 3 times, K5, YO.

Row 7: YO, K5, YO, *(K2tog, YO) 3 times, K2tog, K6, YO; rep from * to 13 sts before marker, (K2tog, YO) 3 times, K2tog, K5, YO.

Row 8: Purl all sts.

Chart B

Row 1 (RS): YO, *3/3 LC, (K2tog, YO) 4 times; rep from * to 6 sts before marker, 3/3 LC, YO.

Row 2 and all even-numbered rows (WS): Purl all sts.

Row 3: YO, K1, *K6, (YO, K2tog) 4 times; rep from * to 7 sts before marker, K7, YO.

Row 5: YO, K2, *K7, (YO, K2tog) 3 times, K1; rep from * to 8 sts before marker, K8, YO.

Row 7: YO, K3, *K2, YO, K2tog, K4, (YO, K2tog) twice, K2; rep from * to 9 sts before marker, K2, YO, K2tog, K5, YO.

Row 9: YO, K4, *K1, (YO, K2tog) twice, K4, YO, K2tog, K3; rep from * to 10 sts before marker, K1, (YO, K2tog) twice, K5, YO.

Row 11: YO, K5, *(YO, K2tog) 3 times, K8; rep from * to 11 sts before marker, (YO, K2tog) 3 times, K5, YO.

Row 13: YO, K5, YO, *(K2tog, YO) 3 times, K2tog, K6, YO; rep from * to 13 sts before marker, (K2tog, YO) 3 times, K2tog, K5, YO.

Row 14: Purl all sts.

Rep rows 1–14 for patt.

Chart C

Row 1 (RS): YO, K5, YO, K2tog, *(YO, K2tog) 4 times, K4, YO, K2tog; rep from * to 13 sts before marker, (YO, K2tog) 4 times, K5, YO.

Rows 2 and 4 (WS): Purl all sts.

Row 3: YO, K5, YO, K2tog, YO, *(K2tog, YO) 4 times, K2tog, K2, YO, K2tog, YO; rep from * to 15 sts before marker, (K2tog, YO) 4 times, K2tog, K5, YO.

Row 5: YO, K5, (YO, K2tog) to 5 sts before marker, K5, YO.

Row 6: Purl all sts.

Wanderer chart A

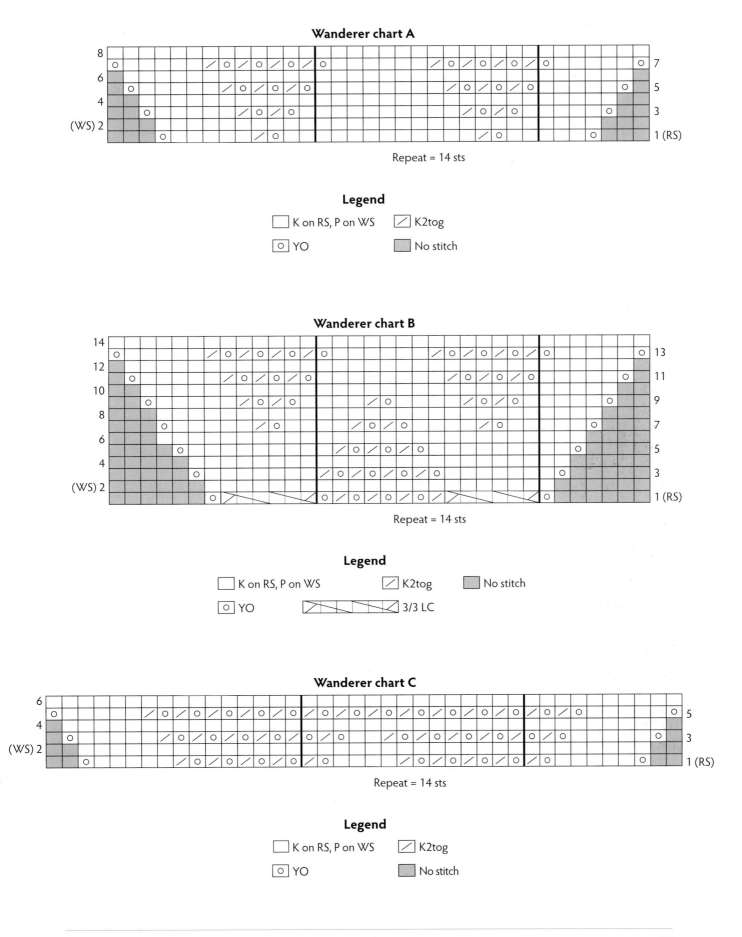

Repeat = 14 sts

Legend

☐ K on RS, P on WS   ╱ K2tog

◯ YO   ▨ No stitch

Wanderer chart B

Repeat = 14 sts

Legend

☐ K on RS, P on WS   ╱ K2tog   ▨ No stitch

◯ YO   ⧅ 3/3 LC

Wanderer chart C

Repeat = 14 sts

Legend

☐ K on RS, P on WS   ╱ K2tog

◯ YO   ▨ No stitch

GRIVOLA

Designed and knit by author

A garter-stitch lace border with striking peaks and valleys graces the edge of this simple sideways shawl. Worked in one piece, this bulky shawl is quick to knit.

SKILL LEVEL: Easy

FINISHED MEASUREMENTS: 14" x 60"

MATERIALS

3 skeins of Alpine Wool from Lion Brand (100% wool; 85 g; 93 yards) in color 174 Olive (**5**)

US size 10½ (6.5 mm) circular needle, 24" cable or longer, or size required for gauge

1 stitch marker

Tapestry needle

Blocking supplies

GAUGE

12 sts and 20 rows = 4" in garter st

Gauge is not critical in this patt, but a different gauge will affect yardage and size of shawl.

PATTERN NOTES

Chart is on page 79. If you prefer to follow written instructions for the charted material, see "Written Instructions for Chart" on page 79.

On row 11, after binding off 5 sts, there is 1 st on RH needle. This counts as the first st worked after the sts are bound off (i.e., it's the first st of the K9 that follows the binding off).

INSTRUCTIONS

CO 11 sts.

Set-up row (WS): K2, PM, K9.

Increase Section

Row 1 (RS): Work row 1 of chart to marker, SM, M1, knit to end.

Row 2 (WS): Knit to marker, SM, work row 2 of chart to end.

Binding off stitches in the lace border every 12 rows adds interest at the edge.

Row 3: Work row 3 of chart to marker, SM, knit to end.

Row 4: Knit to marker, SM, work row 4 of chart to end.

Row 5: Work row 5 of chart to marker, SM, M1, knit to end.

Row 6: Knit to marker, SM, work row 6 of chart to end.

Row 7: Work row 7 of chart to marker, SM, knit to end.

Row 8: Knit to marker, SM, work row 8 of chart to end.

Row 9: Work row 9 of chart to marker, SM, M1, knit to end.

Row 10: Knit to marker, SM, work row 10 of chart to end.

Row 11: Work row 11 of chart to marker, SM, knit to end.

Row 12: Knit to marker, SM, work row 12 of chart to end.

Rep last 12 rows another 7 times—35 sts total (9 sts from chart, 26 sts in garter-st body).

Straight Section

Row 1 (RS): Work row 1 of chart to marker, SM, knit to end.

Row 2 (WS): Knit to marker, SM, work row 2 of chart to end.

Row 3: Work row 3 of chart to marker, SM, knit to end.

Row 4: Knit to marker, SM, work row 4 of chart to end.

Row 5: Work row 5 of chart to marker, SM, knit to end.

Row 6: Knit to marker, SM, work row 6 of chart to end.

Row 7: Work row 7 of chart to marker, SM, knit to end.

Row 8: Knit to marker, SM, work row 8 of chart to end.

Row 9: Work row 9 of chart to marker, SM, knit to end.

Row 10: Knit to marker, SM, work row 10 of chart to end.

Row 11: Work row 11 of chart to marker, SM, knit to end.

Row 12: Knit to marker, SM, work row 12 of chart to end.

Rep last 12 rows another 4 times.

Decrease Section

Row 1 (RS): Work row 1 of chart to marker, SM, K2tog, knit to end.

Row 2 (WS): Knit to marker, SM, work row 2 of chart to end.

Row 3: Work row 3 of chart to marker, SM, knit to end.

Row 4: Knit to marker, SM, work row 4 of chart to end.

Row 5: Work row 5 of chart to marker, SM, K2tog, knit to end.

Row 6: Knit to marker, SM, work row 6 of chart to end.

Row 7: Work row 7 of chart to marker, SM, knit to end.

Row 8: Knit to marker, SM, work row 8 of chart to end.

Row 9: Work row 9 of chart to marker, SM, K2tog, knit to end.

Row 10: Knit to marker, SM, work row 10 of chart to end.

Row 11: Work row 11 of chart to marker, SM, knit to end.

Row 12: Knit to marker, SM, work row 12 of chart to end.

Rep last 12 rows another 7 times—11 sts total (9 sts from chart, 2 sts in garter-st body).

FINISHING

BO loosely kw (page 91) on RS. Block shawl to finished measurements given at beg of patt. With tapestry needle, weave in ends.

WRITTEN INSTRUCTIONS FOR CHART

If you prefer to follow row-by-row written instructions rather than a chart, use the following instructions.

Row 1 (RS): K2, (YO, K2tog) twice, YO, K3—10 sts.

Row 2 and all even-numbered rows: Knit all sts.

Row 3: K2, (YO, K2tog) twice, YO, K4—11 sts.

Row 5: K2, (YO, K2tog) twice, YO, K5—12 sts.

Row 7: K2, (YO, K2tog) twice, YO, K6—13 sts.

Row 9: K2, (YO, K2tog) twice, YO, K7—14 sts.

Row 11: BO 5 sts, K9—9 sts.

Row 12: Knit all sts.

Rep rows 1–12 for patt.

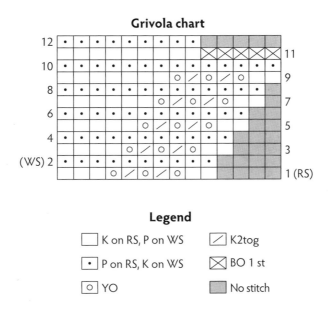

Grivola chart

Legend

☐ K on RS, P on WS

• P on RS, K on WS

○ YO

╱ K2tog

☒ BO 1 st

▨ No stitch

LACON

Designed and knit by author

Ribbing flows perfectly into winding cables on this chunky cowl. This piece is worked in the round and will be finished in a flash—no matter which version you choose to knit.

SKILL LEVEL: Intermediate

SIZES: Cowl (Infinity Scarf)

FINISHED CIRCUMFERENCE:
25 (54)", slightly stretched

FINISHED DEPTH: 10"

MATERIALS

2 (3) skeins of Tosh Chunky
   from Madelinetosh (100%
   superwash merino wool;
   100 g; 165 yards) in color
   Fragrant (**5**)
US size 9 (5.5 mm) circular
   needle, 16 (32)" cable, or
   size required for gauge

Cable needle
1 stitch marker
Tapestry needle
Blocking supplies

GAUGE

14 sts and 24 rows = 4" in
reverse St st

SPECIAL ABBREVIATIONS

2/2 RC: Sl 2 sts to cable needle,
hold in back, K2, K2 from cable
needle

2/2 LC: Sl 2 sts to cable needle,
hold in front, K2, K2 from cable
needle

PATTERN NOTES

Chart is on page 83. If you
prefer to follow written
instructions for the charted
material, see "Written
Instructions for Chart" on
page 82.

Pattern is written for cowl with
instructions for infinity scarf
written in parentheses, where
necessary. If only one
instruction is given, it should
be worked for both versions.
Infinity scarf is shown.

Make It Your Own!

Adjust the circumference of the cowl by adding or subtracting stitches in multiples of 18 (i.e., 18, 36, 54, etc.). Adjusting the size will affect the amount of yarn you will need. Also, try experimenting with different weights of yarn with this pattern. As long as you cast on a multiple of 18 sts, you can create the size cowl you want.

INSTRUCTIONS

CO 90 (198) sts. Join in the round, being careful not to twist sts. PM to mark beg of rnd.

Ribbing rnd: *K2, P3, K4, P1, K4, P3, K1; rep from * to end of rnd.

Rep ribbing rnd for another 6 rnds (7 rnds total).

Work rnds 1–28 of chart. Work rnds 1–22 once more.

Work ribbing rnd for 7 rnds.

FINISHING

BO loosely in patt. Block cowl to finished measurements given at beg of patt. With tapestry needle, weave in ends.

WRITTEN INSTRUCTIONS FOR CHART

If you prefer to follow row-by-row written instructions rather than a chart, use the following instructions.

Rnd 1: *P4, K2tog, K3, YO, P1, YO, K3, ssk, P3; rep from * to end of rnd.

Rnd 2: *P4, (K4, P3) twice; rep from * to end of rnd.

Rnd 3: *P3, K2tog, K3, YO, P3, YO, K3, ssk, P2; rep from * to end of rnd.

Rnd 4: *P3, K4, P5, K4, P2; rep from * to end of rnd.

Rnd 5: *P2, K2tog, K3, YO, P5, YO, K3, ssk, P1; rep from * to end of rnd.

Rnd 6: *P2, K4, P7, K4, P1; rep from * to end of rnd.

Rnd 7: *P1, K2tog, K3, YO, P7, YO, K3, ssk; rep from * to end of rnd.

Rnd 8: *P1, K4, P9, K4; rep from * to end of rnd.

Rnd 9: *P1, 2/2 LC, P9, 2/2 RC; rep from * to end of rnd.

Rnds 10–12: *P1, K4, P9, K4; rep from * to end of rnd.

Rnd 13: Rep rnd 9.

Rnd 14: *P1, K4, P9, K4; rep from * to end of rnd.

Rnd 15: *P1, YO, K3, ssk, P7, K2tog, K3, YO; rep from * to end of rnd.

Rnd 16: Rep rnd 6.

Rnd 17: *P2, YO, K3, ssk, P5, K2tog, K3, YO, P1; rep from * to end of rnd.

Rnd 18: Rep rnd 4.

Rnd 19: *P3, YO, K3, ssk, P3, K2tog, K3, YO, P2; rep from * to end of rnd.

Rnd 20: Rep rnd 2.

The traveling cable creates an interesting lattice pattern throughout the cowl. Reverse stockinette stitch is the perfect background to make these cables pop.

Rnd 21: *P4, YO, K3, ssk, P1, K2tog, K3, YO, P3; rep from * to end of rnd.

Rnd 22: *P5, K4, P1, K4, P4; rep from * to end of rnd.

Rnd 23: *P5, 2/2 LC, P1, 2/2 RC, P4; rep from * to end of rnd.

Rnds 24–26: *P5, K4, P1, K4, P4; rep from * to end of rnd.

Rnd 27: Rep rnd 23.

Rnd 28: Rep rnd 22.

Rep rnds 1–28 for patt.

Lacon chart

																		28
																		27
																		26
																		25
																		24
																		23
																		22
																		21
																		20
																		19
																		18
																		17
																		16
																		15
																		14
																		13
																		12
																		11
																		10
																		9
																		8
																		7
																		6
																		5
																		4
																		3
																		2
																		1

Repeat = 18 sts

Legend

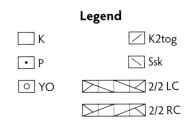

□	K	╱	K2tog
•	P	╲	Ssk
○	YO		2/2 LC
			2/2 RC

VINIFERA

Designed and knit by author

A reverse stockinette stitch is the perfect background to make a lace leaf motif pop. Small eyelet details add extra interest to this relaxed-fitting hat.

SKILL LEVEL: Experienced

FINISHED CIRCUMFERENCE: 20", fits up to 23"

FINISHED HEIGHT: 9"

MATERIALS

1 skein of Tundra from The Fibre Company (60% baby alpaca, 30% merino wool, 10% silk; 100 g; 120 yards) in color 623 Aurora
US size 9 (5.5 mm) circular needle, 16" cable, or size required for gauge

Set of 5 double-pointed needles in US size 9 (5.5 mm), or size required for gauge
1 stitch marker
Tapestry needle

GAUGE

12 sts and 20 rows = 4" in rev St st

PATTERN NOTES

Chart is on page 86. If you prefer written instructions for the charted material, see "Written Instructions for Chart" on page 86.

INSTRUCTIONS

With circular needle, CO 68 sts. Join in the round, being careful not to twist sts. PM to mark start of rnd.

Ribbing rnd: *K1, P2, K2, P3, K1, P3, K2, P2, K1; rep from * to end of rnd.

Work ribbing rnd for another 11 rnds (12 rnds total).

Work chart one time (16 rnds).

Next rnd: *(K1, P7) twice, K1; rep from * to end of rnd.

Rep last rnd another 3 times.

Dec as follows:

Note: Switch to dpns when stitches no longer comfortably fit on 16" circular.

Rnd 1: *K1, ssp, P5, K1, P5, P2tog, K1; rep from * to end of rnd—60 sts.

Rnd 2: *(K1, P6) twice, K1; rep from * to end of rnd.

Rnd 3: *K1, ssp, P4, K1, P4, P2tog, K1; rep from * to end of rnd—52 sts.

Rnd 4: *(K1, P5) twice, K1; rep from * to end of rnd.

Rnd 5: *K1, ssp, P3, K1, P3, P2tog, K1; rep from * to end of rnd—44 sts.

Rnd 6: *K1, ssp, P2, K1, P2, P2tog, K1; rep from * to end of rnd—36 sts.

Rnd 7: *K1, ssp, P1, K1, P1, P2tog, K1; rep from * to end of rnd—28 sts.

Rnd 8: *K1, ssp, K1, P2tog, K1; rep from * to end of rnd—20 sts.

Rnd 9: *K1, CDD, K1; rep from * to end of rnd—12 sts.

FINISHING

Cut yarn, leaving 8" tail. Thread yarn onto tapestry needle and thread through rem sts. Gather sts and tie off. Weave in ends.

WRITTEN INSTRUCTIONS FOR CHART

If you prefer to follow row-by-row written instructions rather than a chart, use the following instructions.

Rnd 1: *K1, ssp, P5, YO, K1, YO, P5, P2tog, K1; rep from * to end of rnd.

Rnd 2: *K1, P6, K3, P6, K1; rep from * to end of rnd.

Rnd 3: *K1, ssp, P4, (K1, YO) twice, K1, P4, P2tog, K1; rep from * to end of rnd.

Rnd 4: *K1, P5, K5, P5, K1; rep from * to end of rnd.

Rnd 5: *K1, ssp, P3, K2, YO, K1, YO, K2, P3, P2tog, K1; rep from * to end of rnd.

Rnd 6: *K1, P4, K7, P4, K1; rep from * to end of rnd.

Rnd 7: *K1, ssp, P2, K3, YO, K1, YO, K3, P2, P2tog, K1; rep from * to end of rnd.

Rnd 8: *K1, P3, K9, P3, K1; rep from * to end of rnd.

Rnd 9: *K1, P1, YO, P2, K3, CDD, K3, P2, YO, P1, K1; rep from * to end of rnd.

Rnd 10: Rep rnd 6.

Rnd 11: *K1, P1, YO, P3, K2, CDD, K2, P3, YO, P1, K1; rep from * to end of rnd.

Rnd 12: Rep rnd 4.

Rnd 13: *K1, P1, YO, P4, K1, CDD, K1, P4, YO, P1, K1; rep from * to end of rnd.

Rnd 14: Rep rnd 2.

Rnd 15: *K1, P1, YO, P5, CDD, P5, YO, P1, K1; rep from * to end of rnd.

Rnd 16: *(K1, P7) twice, K1; rep from * to end of rnd.

Vinifera chart

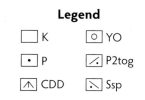

Repeat = 17 sts

Legend

☐	K	○	YO
•	P	╱	P2tog
⋏	CDD	╲	Ssp

REMY

Designed and knit by author

The simple chevrons in this cowl give you the opportunity to play with different types of yarn. This piece looks great in a heathered yarn as shown in the featured cowl, or it can be just as pretty in a variegated yarn.

SKILL LEVEL: Intermediate

SIZES: Cowl (Infinity Scarf)

FINISHED CIRCUMFERENCE: 24 (48)", slightly stretched

FINISHED LENGTH: 8"

MATERIALS

1 (2) skeins of Ultra Alpaca Chunky from Berroco (50% super fine alpaca, 50% Peruvian wool; 100 g; 131 yards) in color 72171 Berry Pie Mix (**5**)

US size 10 (6.0 mm) circular needle, 16 (32)" cable, or size required for gauge
1 stitch marker
Tapestry needle
Blocking supplies

GAUGE

14 sts and 20 rows = 4" in St st

PATTERN NOTES

Chart is on page 89. If you prefer to follow written instructions for the charted material, see "Written Instructions for Chart" on page 89.

Pattern is written for cowl with instructions for infinity scarf written in parentheses, where necessary. If only one instruction is given, it should be worked for both versions. Cowl is shown.

INSTRUCTIONS

CO 84 (168) sts. Join in the round, being careful not to twist sts. PM to mark beg of rnd.

Ribbing rnd: *K2, P1; rep from * to end of rnd.

Rep ribbing rnd for another 2 rnds (3 rnds total).

Make It Your Own!

You can adjust the circumference by adding or subtracting stitches in multiples of 12 (i.e., 12, 24, 36, etc.). Adjusting the size will affect the amount of yarn you will need. Also, you can experiment with different weights of yarn with this pattern. As long as you cast on a multiple of 12 sts, you can create the size cowl you want!

Work rnds 1 and 2 of chart until piece measures 7" from CO edge, ending with rnd 2.

Work ribbing rnd for 3 rnds.

FINISHING

BO loosely in patt. Block cowl to finished measurements given at beg of patt. With tapestry needle, weave in ends.

WRITTEN INSTRUCTIONS FOR CHART

If you prefer to follow row-by-row written instructions rather than a chart, use the following instructions.

Rnd 1: *K2tog, K3, M1, K1, M1, K3, ssk, P1; rep from * to end of rnd.

Rnd 2: *K11, P1; rep from * to end of rnd.

Rep rnds 1 and 2 for patt.

A textured chevron pattern makes this a perfect project for all different types of yarn.

Remy chart

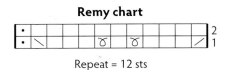

Repeat = 12 sts

Legend

□ K   ╱ K2tog

• P   ╲ Ssk

⅀ M1

Special Techniques

The following techniques are used throughout the book and will help you successfully knit your projects.

GARTER-TAB CAST ON

Several projects in this book begin with a garter-tab cast on. This cast on is typically worked as follows.

1. Cast on three stitches and knit six rows.

2. Rotate work clockwise 90° and pick up three stitches evenly along the edge. Try to insert the needle into each of the three bumps on the edge of the tab.

3. Rotate work clockwise 90° and pick up three stitches evenly from the cast-on edge (nine stitches total). Turn your work and continue with row 1 of the pattern.

KNITTED CAST ON

Use this cast on to add extra stitches to a shawl, typically when working a border. Start with a slipknot on the left-hand needle. Insert the right-hand needle into the slipknot as if to knit, yarn over, and pull a loop through. Transfer the new stitch from the right-hand needle to the left-hand needle.

Knit into the last stitch on the left-hand needle and transfer the new stitch back to the left-hand needle until you have the correct number of stitches.

KNITWISE BIND OFF

You can bind off your project in a number of different ways. For a shawl, the goal is to have a bind off that's stretchy so that when blocking the shawl, you can pull and form the edge any way you like. For other projects, like fingerless mitts, you want the bind off to be loose enough to fit over your hand when finished. The following is my favorite knitwise bind off. If you tend to bind off tightly, try using a needle one or two sizes larger.

To work, knit the first two stitches together through the back loop. *Slip the stitch from the right needle to the left needle with the yarn in back and knit two together through the back loops; repeat from * until all stitches are bound off.

Yarn Weight and Substitutions

One question I frequently receive from knitters concerns yarn weight and substitutions. When it comes to accessories (like scarves and shawls) that don't need to have a specific fit, it's usually pretty easy to switch to a thinner or thicker yarn, depending on your preference. However, there are a few things you need to consider when changing the weight of yarn for your project.

First, think about how the item needs to fit. For example, the Merope fingerless mitts (page 35) are worked in a DK-weight yarn. If you were to switch to a bulky-weight yarn, use the appropriate needle for that yarn, and knit Merope as written, you would end up with mitts that would fit something much larger than a human adult! The pattern can be adapted for a different weight of yarn, but there's going to be swatching and math involved. However, when it comes to shawls and scarves, making a change in yarn weight is much simpler. It will change the finished size of the piece, but that isn't as critical as with projects that need to really fit, like mittens or a hat.

The next consideration is how changing the yarn weight is going to affect the size of the finished item. To get a better understanding, let's compare DK-weight, worsted-weight, and bulky-weight yarns.

I used each of these yarns and knit a swatch. For each swatch, I used a needle within the recommended needle range given on the ball band for the yarn. All three swatches were worked as follows:

CO 25 sts. Knit 3 rows.

Row 1 (RS): Knit all sts.

Row 2 (WS): K2, purl to last 2 sts, K2.

Rep rows 1 and 2 for a total of 28 rows. Knit 4 rows. BO kw on RS.

You can easily see that the thicker the yarn, the larger the swatch.

From looking at the swatches, it's clear that if we use a thicker yarn and needle than the pattern recommends, and then knit the pattern as written,

From left to right: DK weight, worsted, bulky

From left to right: DK-, worsted-, bulky-weight swatches

the item will end up being larger than the measurements given in the pattern.

That's good information to have, but the next consideration is this: Did we use more yarn on the bulky swatch? Yes! How do we know? Math! Let's compare the DK-weight swatch to the bulky-weight swatch to get a handle on yarn amount used.

The ball band on the DK-weight yarn states that it contains 225 yards and is 100 grams. I can calculate the yards per gram as follows:

225 yards / 100 grams = 2.25 yards per gram

I knit my swatch and then weighed it. The DK-weight swatch weighed 10 grams. I now multiply the weight of the swatch (10 grams) by the yards-per-gram result.

10 grams x 2.25 yards per gram = 22.5 yards

I know that I used 22.5 yards in my DK-weight swatch. Now we can repeat the process for the bulky swatch. The ball band on the bulky-weight yarn indicates that there are 165 yards in the skein for 100 grams. Using the first equation above, we can determine that bulky yarn has 1.65 yards per gram. My completed swatch weighs 20 grams. Using the second equation, we can calculate that I used 33 yards for my bulky swatch. When working a pattern the same way for a DK-weight and bulky yarn, the bulky yarn will use more yarn and result in a larger finished piece!

So play around and experiment with different yarn weights on some of the projects—there are lots of shawls, scarves, and cowls to try! Be on the lookout for those tip boxes, where I'll tell you which patterns are easy to adapt to your yarn choice.

A Note about Gauge

All gauges listed in this book are based on a washed, blocked swatch. Take the time to check the gauge so you don't run out of yarn!

Resources

Refer to the websites of the following companies to find retail shops that carry yarns featured in this book.

Anzula Luxury Fibers
www.anzula.com
Cricket
Cole
For Better or Worsted

Berroco
www.berroco.com
Vintage DK
Vintage Chunky
Ultra Alpaca Chunky

Blue Sky Alpacas
www.blueskyalpacas.com
Extra

Fiberstory
www.fiberstory.net
Core DK

The Fibre Company
www.thefibreco.com
Canopy Worsted
Tundra

Hazel Knits
www.hazelknits.com
Lively DK
Cadence

Imperial Yarn
www.imperialyarn.com
Erin

Knit Picks
www.knitpicks.com
City Tweed DK
Wool of the Andes
      Superwash Bulky

Lion Brand Yarns
www.lionbrand.com
Wool-Ease
Alpine Wool

Madelinetosh Yarns
www.madelinetosh.com
Tosh DK
Tosh Chunky

Shalimar Yarns
www.shalimaryarns.com
Breathless DK

Spud & Chloe
www.spudandchloe.com
Outer

String Theory Hand Dyed Yarn
www.stringtheoryyarn.com
Merino DK

Useful Information

Yarn-Weight Symbol and Category Name	(1) Super Fine	(2) Fine	(3) Light	(4) Medium	(5) Bulky	(6) Super Bulky
Types of Yarn in Category	Sock, Fingering, Baby	Sport, Baby	DK, Light Worsted	Worsted, Afghan, Aran	Chunky, Craft, Rug	Bulky, Roving
Knit Gauge Range* in Stockinette Stitch to 4"	27 to 32 sts	23 to 26 sts	21 to 24 sts	16 to 20 sts	12 to 15 sts	6 to 11 sts
Recommended Needle in US Size Range	1 to 3	3 to 5	5 to 7	7 to 9	9 to 11	11 and larger
Recommended Needle in Metric Size Range	2.25 to 3.25 mm	3.25 to 3.75 mm	3.75 to 4.5 mm	4.5 to 5.5 mm	5.5 to 8 mm	8 mm and larger

These are guidelines only. The above reflect the most commonly used gauges and needles for specific yarn categories.

KNITTING NEEDLE SIZES

US Size	Size in Millimeters
1	2.25 mm
2	2.75 mm
3	3.25 mm
4	3.5 mm
5	3.75 mm
6	4 mm
7	4.5 mm
8	5 mm
9	5.5 mm
10	6 mm
10½	6.5 mm
11	8 mm
13	9 mm
15	10 mm
17	12.75 mm
19	15 mm
35	19 mm
50	25 mm

METRIC CONVERSION

Yards	=	meters	x	1.0936
Meters	=	yards	x	0.9144
Ounces	=	grams	x	0.0352
Grams	=	ounces	x	28.35

SKILL LEVELS

Easy: Projects using basic stitches, repetitive stitch patterns, and simple color changes; simple shaping and finishing.

Intermediate: Projects using a variety of stitches, such as basic cables and lace, simple intarsia, and techniques for double-pointed needles and knitting in the round; mid-level shaping and finishing.

Experienced: Projects using advanced techniques and stitches, such as short rows, Fair Isle, more intricate intarsia, cables, lace patterns, and numerous color changes.

Knitting Abbreviations

[ ] Work instructions within brackets as many times as directed.

( ) Work instructions within parentheses in the place directed.

* Repeat instructions following the single asterisk as directed.

" inch(es)

approx approximately

beg begin(ning)

BO bind off

CDD slip 2 stitches together as if to knit 2 together, knit 1 stitch, pass the 2 slipped stitches over the knit stitch—2 stitches decreased

cn cable needle(s)

CO cast on

cont continue(ing)(s)

dec decrease(ing)(s)

dpn(s) double-pointed needle(s)

foll follow(ing)

g gram(s)

inc(s) increase(ing)(s)

K knit

K1f&b knit into the front and back of the next stitch—1 stitch increased

K2tog knit 2 stitches together—1 stitch decreased

K3tog knit 3 stitches together—2 stitches decreased

K4tog knit 4 stitches together—3 stitches decreased

kw knitwise

LH left hand

M1 make 1 stitch

M1L make 1 left

M1R make 1 right

P purl

P2tog purl 2 stitches together

patt(s) pattern(s)

PM place marker

pw purlwise

rem remain(ing)

rep(s) repeat(s)

rev reverse

RH right hand

rnd(s) round(s)

RS right side

sk2p slip 1 stitch purlwise, knit 2 stitches together, pass slipped stitch over, K2tog—2 stitches decreased

sl slip

sl st(s) slip stitch(es)

SM slip marker

ssk slip 2 stitches knitwise, 1 at a time, to right needle, then insert left needle from left to right into front loops and knit 2 stitches together—1 stitch decreased

ssp slip 2 stitches knitwise, 1 at a time, to right needle, slip stitches back to left needle, and purl 2 stitches together through back loops—1 stitch decreased

sssk slip 3 stitches knitwise, 1 at a time, to right needle, then insert left needle from left to right into front loops and knit 3 stitches together—2 stitches decreased

ssssk slip 4 stitches knitwise, 1 at a time, to right needle, then insert left needle from left to right into front loops and knit 4 stitches together—3 stitches decreased

st(s) stitch(es)

St st(s) stockinette stitch(es)

tbl through back loop

tog together

WS wrong side

wyib with yarn in back

wyif with yarn in front

YO(s) yarn over(s)

Acknowledgments

Working on a book is definitely a group effort, and I'm so lucky to have such wonderful people as part of my team. Thank you to my sample knitters, Jenni Lesniak, Cathy Rusk, and Melissa Rusk. I'm deeply grateful for all your hard work in bringing this book together. To my knit and crochet group, thank you for being a wonderful resource for discussing ideas for this book and for encouraging me to keep going even when things were tough.

Thank you to the entire Martingale team. You have been a dream to work with, and I look forward to our continued endeavors together.

As always, thank you to my husband, Alex. I couldn't do this without your support.

About the Author

Jen has been knitting since 2004 and designing since 2008. Her designs have been seen in several magazines, including *Interweave Knits, Knitscene,* and *Love of Knitting.* She is the author of the popular *Sock-Yarn Shawls* books, and you can also find dozens of her self-published patterns on Ravelry. In 2014, after a decade of testing municipal wastewater for a living, she retired her lab coat and safety glasses to work in her design business full-time. When she's not knitting, you can find Jen crocheting, reading, or trying new slow-cooker recipes she found online. She lives in Fox River Grove, Illinois, with her husband, Alex.

FIND JEN ONLINE!

See Jen's designs at www.ravelry.com/designers/jen-lucas.

Check out Jen's website at www.jenlucasdesigns.com.

Follow Jen on Twitter and Instagram @knitlikecrazy.